IN $\mathcal{S}$ICKNESS &
IN $\mathcal{H}$EALTH

One Woman's Story of Love, Loss, and Healing

BY GAIL LYNCH

Fairview Press, Minneapolis

Published by Fairview Press, 2450 Riverside Avenue, Minneapolis, Minnesota 55454. Fairview Press is a division of Fairview Health Services, a community-focused health system providing a complete range of services, from the prevention of illness and injury to care for the most complex medical conditions.

Library of Congress Cataloging-in-Publication Data
Lynch, Gail, 1942-
    In Sickness and in health : one woman's story of love, loss, and healing / Gail Lynch
      p. cm.
  ISBN 1-57749-113-0 (pbk. : alk. paper)
    1. Mansoldo, Raymond Robert, 1941--Health. 2. Lynch, Gail, 1942- 3. Brain--Cancer--Patients--United States--Biography. 4. Widows--United States--Biography. I. Title.

RC280.B7 M3655 2002
362.1'9699481'0092--dc21   2001040664
[B]

First Printing: January 2002
Printed in the United States
05 04 03 02   6 5 4 3 2 1

The poem on page 116 reprinted with the permission of Simon & Schuster, Inc., from "Strange Holiness" by Robert P. Tristam Coffin. Copyright © 1935 by Macmillan Publishing Company, copyright renewed © 1963 by Margaret Coffin Halvosa.

Cover design by Laurie Ingram

For a free current catalog of Fairview Press titles, please call toll-free 1-800-544-8207. Or visit our Web site at www.fairviewpress.org.

For Bob, of course

ACKNOWLEDGMENTS

One of the wonderful things about writing a book is that it gives me a public forum in which to acknowledge the many people who have supported me over the years.

I am grateful to Lane Stiles, director of Fairview Press, and to Stephanie Billecke, senior editor. Their kindness and quick responses to my e-mails assured me that my book was in good hands. Everyone should be lucky enough to have an editor like Stephanie, who can not only make the book better, but will also make the editing process fun. I am grateful as well to my former agent at ICM, Mitch Douglas, who never wavered in his support of my writing. I owe a lot also to Nancy Kelton and her Wednesday night writing group—specifically Michele Bender, Michele Fillion, Ellen Zimmerman, Michael Koegel, and Margie Goldsmith—who listened to this book, five pages at a time, and offered gentle, helpful feedback.

To Bob's family, every member providing support in his or her own way, I am grateful. And to my own family—my sons, Chris and Tim Lynch; daughter-in-law, Lisa Hazard; future daughter-in-law, Nancy Ng; cousin, Lee Glenn; and brother, Bill Oberlin—I want to say a special thanks for your steadfast love and support.

I am also indebted to my therapists, official and unofficial: Jeff Pusar, Bess Bonness, Edie Berke, and Pat Harris, whose gifts are listening, reframing, and truly understanding. Thanks also to the Pru Cru for adopting me. My appreciation also goes to Kira

Gray, who helped me find rainbows at the Maui Writers Retreat, and to Jerry Bozman, who introduced me to a healthy lifestyle, beginning with running, meditation, and never again eating cheesecake. My many friends—those mentioned in the book, and those who weren't—have all added to my life in ways I couldn't even begin to enumerate.

Finally, I want to acknowledge all caregivers. There is no more important task. I am grateful and honored to have been there.

PART ONE

ONE

How many widows does it take to change a light bulb? One—and a ladder, a step stool, a ten-foot pole, entreaties to God, a lot of four-letter words, a fear of broken bones, and a sprinkle of tears. How could it have happened that Bob is no longer here to drag the ladder across the yard and climb the tall oak tree to replace a floodlight?

"Do you smell something funny?" He held an uncapped pen under my nose.

"No, it just smells like a regular pen," I said.

This was Bob's fourth reality check of the day. We had spent the last twelve hours on planes and in airports, and so far we had only managed to get from New Jersey to Chicago, the first leg of our trip to Arizona.

"Smell it again," he said, then closed his eyes. For a few seconds he paled and faded out.

When we finally got to Sedona the next afternoon, I pleaded with Bob's brother Roger to take us to a doctor. "We think it's his allergies again, or maybe he's taking too much of the allergy medication. He's been doing that now, since we got Lucky."

Got Lucky. There's a figure of speech for you. How were we to know that we had decidedly *not* gotten lucky? Our new kitten was Lucky, not us.

Bob hated doctors. He never went without a battle. Doctors do awful things to you. They stick needles into you and draw blood out of you and do other things to invade your private self. But this time he went without a fight.

The doctor took his time, did all kinds of tests, took a complete history, and finally changed Bob's allergy medication. He had been taking the wrong medication, and too much of it. Normally, Bob was as conservative about new medications as he was about any other kind of change. He had had the same prescription for twenty years—why should he change now? But this time he did what the doctor said.

At the end of our visit, the physician suggested that we go to our own doctor back in New Jersey. Bob, of course, didn't have one. "If this new medication works, do you think we should still go?" I asked.

"Well, I think you might want a CAT scan or an MRI to rule out something more serious."

"Like what?" I did the talking in doctors' offices.

"Like a brain tumor."

Both Bob and I had heard him, but we didn't ask any more questions. We tried the new medication. No more funny smells, no more blackouts. No reason to worry. Except for the asthma, Bob was very healthy. He hadn't missed a day of work in years. Whenever I had a cold he would kiss me and say, "It's okay. I never get sick."

Bob was quieter than usual, contemplative. He wasn't smiling often these days and frequently seemed close to tears. On a gut level he was able to recognize that something was wrong enough for him to follow a doctor's orders. From the time he was three years old, he had run and hidden if there was any hint that he might end up in a doctor's office. But this time, either he had run out of hiding places or his more rational—or maybe more fearful—self won out. When we got back to New Jersey, we went to the doctor.

Bob and I had been husband and wife eleven years. My sons, Tim and Chris, were fourteen and ten when we got married. At the time Chris reminded me, "You said you were never getting married again." Tim added, "You can do better than him, Mom."

But how can you not marry a man who wakes up next to you each morning, telling you that meeting you was the best day of his whole life? How can you not marry someone whose first gift to you is to clean up your driveway and buy you a new garbage can to go with it? And how can you not marry the man who listens patiently to your diatribe about a colleague at work and then says, "Are you done yet? I'm getting mad at her now, too." And how can you not marry a man who, in the middle of an argument when you are just barely speaking to each other, still picks up your son to take him to the library when you have to work late?

We sat in the neurologist's office. The doctor was a natty little man dressed in European style. I had recently learned, as had the rest of the world, that O.J. Simpson wore Bruno Magli shoes. I guessed that maybe that's what the doctor wore, too. He was polished. When he told us that the MRI he had ordered would have to be read by someone covering for him, Bob asked him where he was going on vacation. He wouldn't tell us. Surely he didn't think we'd try to call or follow him.

By now there were more symptoms—splitting headaches, vomiting, and, one day, after an uncharacteristic nap, Bob said, "Fish. The green makes time. Bones the farther." I looked at him, aghast. He knew I didn't understand a word he had said—it was like trying to decipher a schizophrenic's word salad—but he couldn't do a damn thing about it except look at me, puzzled. I was sure he had a blocked carotid artery and there wasn't enough oxygen getting to the brain.

The next day I held Bob's watch and wedding ring while he was fed through the MRI tube. In the waiting room he had held my hand, as he always did, and the receptionist asked if he needed me in the examination room with him. He said he thought he would be a big boy and try it without me. This bravery was new for him. While he was held captive in the MRI machine, building security announced that there would be a fire drill. I had to leave the building, glad for Bob's courage in going it alone. We met in the lobby when the test was over. Bob reached for my hand, then put his arm around me for comfort. For both of us.

It was 7:30 P.M. when I got home the next night. I had seen two patients at my psychotherapy practice. I had seen them, literally, but I couldn't remember a word they had said. Bob met me at the door.

"The doctor called. He says I have this thing in my head." Bob's language was oblique sometimes. He didn't name things, as that would make them real. *Brain tumor* was one of those things. *Cancer* was soon to be another.

I called the covering doctor and made an appointment to talk with him in person the next day. Then I picked up the steroids he had prescribed to reduce the brain swelling and the Dilantin to prevent seizures, both of which were common with brain tumors. Bob felt much better after taking the medication. I'd feel better, I thought, after meeting with the doctor. I needed to find out exactly what the diagnosis was. Bob was not going to be a reliable reporter. I could tell.

"It is most likely a glioma, given its size and location," the doctor told us. I was soon going to learn the difference between a glioblastoma, a meningioma, an astrocytoma, and all the other omas—more than I ever wanted to know about brain tumors.

"What does this mean?"

"Well, it is very serious. But they are doing good things with gene therapy nowadays. There are trials that you can look into." That gave us a sliver of hope. More than a sliver.

"It's in kind of a bad place, I'm afraid, the left temporal lobe where the speech center is. I'm going to send you to the best neurosurgeon I know."

TWO

$\mathcal{I}$ watched Bob push a wheelbarrow full of bagged leaves down the street. Our neighbors had offered to mulch them for us. He looked so forlorn and lost. In a few minutes the phone rang and my neighbor said, "Come down for a cup of tea. Bob's here." It was a command, not a suggestion, and I didn't know how to refuse. I walked down and met Bob, who was standing there with tears in his eyes. "Sarah asked me how I was," he said. "I told her." We were all crying then, and it seemed like a cup of tea might not be such a bad idea. Our own private hell was becoming public.

I told a friend. "It's too bad you love him so much," he sighed. What should you do, marry someone you don't like so losing him won't be so bad? That's a little like a cartoon I saw years ago: a bride in a wedding gown standing at the altar, groom at her side, her hair done up in rollers. "But I want to look nice for the reception," she was saying.

How were we going to tell our families? Bob's especially. It was impossible to be direct with Bob's mother. Since his father had died thirty-something years before, Bob's role and that of his two brothers was to shelter their mom from pain. We had to plan. We decided to call Roger first.

"Sammy," Bob said. God knows where he got that nickname, but Sammy it was. "Sammy, I have some really bad news. You know when I went to the doctor out there? Well, there really is something wrong. It wasn't just the allergies. The doctor says I have a brain tumor." There, he said it. That dreaded phrase. "But they can get it out. I'm going to have surgery next week, and this surgeon that I am going to is absolutely the best. I just read all about him in the paper, in fact. He has a wonderful reputation, so I'm sure it'll be okay."

"Have you told Mom?"

"No. I thought maybe you could go over there and be with her when I call so that you can explain and calm her down if she gets upset."

We called the other brother, Ron, next.

"Okay, man, we won't tell anyone about your situation. I'm sure you don't want anyone to know." Who would he tell? We didn't know anyone in Albuquerque.

"It's all right, man." This was a man-to-man talk. "I don't care if people know. I'm not ashamed of it or anything."

Mom, surprisingly, did better than anyone else. "I wish it were me and not him," she told me. "I always felt so terrible when my kids were sick when they were little." I knew what she meant.

I had decided to begin researching all the treatment possibilities on the Internet. Gluing myself to my computer made me feel in control.

My colleague Michael sent me an e-mail: *After you speak to the doctor, go to the main branch of your library; find some sympathetic-looking reference librarian and spill your guts.*

Bob and I divided up the jobs. Mine was to research and read every piece of information I could find on brain tumors. Bob's was to get well.

We met with the neurosurgeon. His office was filled with what looked like signed pictures of Reagan and Nixon. I wasn't quite close enough to see what they said. The neurosurgeon was a man of few words, though they were clear, direct, and spoken with a slight German accent. "If I don't operate very soon you'll be dead in six weeks." When we both started to cry, he looked confused. "You want me to tell you the truth, don't you?" The Nazi doctor was not someone to open up to. He would do the opening up, but only in a technical way. Because the tumor was in the speech center, the neurosurgeon recommended we see a neuropsychologist for some tests. Bob's left-handedness was to his advantage here. The hope was that he might have some areas of speech on both sides of his brain. If so, then the surgeon could resect more aggressively.

We left the neurosurgeon's office and walked toward the car. I was doing all the driving now. Bob could still drive, but we both were feeling shaky about it. Shaky about life in general, really. Bob looked at me as we got on the highway. My hands trembled on the steering wheel.

"I've never before seen you with such sorrow on your face," he said. "I am so sad at what I'm putting you through. I don't know how I would ever handle this if it were you. I could never do what you are doing with the medical stuff." It was true; Bob could not have taken charge. He would have balanced my checkbook, done our laundry, brought meals eight times a day. But he wouldn't have been able to talk to the doctors.

The Nazi doctor did an excellent surgery. Every physician, including him, said so. I had worried that Bob might wake up talking like Pat Buchanan. Actually, I was more worried that Bob might not wake up. I sat for seven hours, trancelike, waiting for my name to be called so that I might speak with the doctor. There was coffee but I couldn't drink it, fearing I'd have to go to the ladies' room. I waited while a doctor came in and told a young father that his wife had cancer and would have to have a hysterectomy. I waited while another doctor told a young woman that her father had to have an emergency appendectomy. I waited and I waited and I waited. Would our doctor talk to me in front of all these other people, too? Would he talk to me at all, or would he just leave me sitting there into the next morning?

"Don't you want me to come to the hospital with you?" my friend Marsha had asked. "Maybe you should call one of your kids? Or what about your brother?"

The only person I wanted sitting with me in the waiting room was lying on the operating table.

Finally I was paged. The doctor exulted, "I got it all. I got the whole tumor out. Your husband is fine. He'll be going to the neurosurgical unit soon. He can talk and understand me. Excellent surgery. Excellent surgery."

I sent an e-mail to my colleagues at work: *Although the tumor was large, malignant, and in a bad place, the surgeon said they got it all. He's very optimistic. Bob will need radiation and chemo, and the recovery may be long, but this is the best I've felt in a long time. Thanks for helping me get through this. Now, if you can just help me get through a month of my visiting in-laws. . . .*

After his surgery, Bob became very emotional and loving toward everyone. Like a brick of vacuum-packed coffee exposed to air, he seemed to soften. Nurses that Bob had never seen before would come into the room, and he'd say, "Isn't she the best? I've invited her to visit us." The physician's assistant came to check him every morning. He couldn't remember her name, but he told her she was the most beautiful woman in the world. And when his tray was delivered at mealtime, he always, politely, invited the aide to share his dinner. I began to suspect that the doctor had done some special kind of surgery that touches on a part of the brain that makes people more sensitive, warm, and loving. I was thinking about getting a referral myself.

E-mail was becoming my favorite and most helpful form of communication. I wrote to Michael: *The neurosurgeon is calling this a glioblastoma multiforme. We will have to wait a little longer for the official pathology report. You may be right that I will find my in-laws more helpful than I think. Under the best of conditions they are very critical. Maybe under the worst of conditions they won't be. People in the office are avoiding me. I haven't told them why I've been out and no one seems to ask. I'm not used to an environment where there is such a hands-off policy about anything personal.*

Michael answered: *I understand about personal issues being avoided. After Greg died, people at work were split into two camps. The first, and by far the largest, were the people who knew he had died but never said a word to me about it. No sorry. No nothing. Maybe it was poor social skills, or maybe just ignorance. Or maybe they truly didn't care. Or, in my case, maybe it's the lifestyle thing. I don't really care. I just find it interesting. The other camp at least acknowledged my loss and didn't avoid me.*

I had known Michael for a few years, but until he had started working in the department that I managed I hadn't had much interaction with him. His office was in Houston and mine was in New Jersey. I certainly hadn't known him on a personal level, known that he had been in a relationship, or known that he had been grieving for a few years. Now I asked him about Greg.

Michael responded: *Greg died of AIDS on December 10, 1994, at 6:15 in the evening. I'm surprised that you didn't hear. I guess I thought you were one of those that didn't want to mention it. I should have known better. He was truly my life partner. Someday when we get together I'll tell you the whole Michael/Greg story regardless of whether or not you want to hear it. For some reason, I find it soothing to talk about this. I feel that I can help others prepare. Let's face it. Everyone dies. I just wasn't ready for my thirty-eight-year-old partner to die.*

THREE

$\mathcal{I}$t was March, the day of Bob's surgery. It had started snowing, a wet sloppy snow, very early in the morning. The snow turned to slush on the streets and made them slippery, reflecting our mood.

The winter had been long, with a major blizzard that had stopped travel for a few days. It had taken weeks for the towering snowdrifts of January to be melted by the sun into dingy gray piles. Even then, the snowstorms continued.

Bob was in the hospital for almost two weeks. When he came home, it was spring. Purple crocuses and snowbells had popped up all over the lawn, and daffodils were just about to follow. "It's great to get home in the spring. A rebirth," he said. Soon the lawn would be glowing with green grass beribboned with fuchsia azaleas.

Bob's brother Ron had been the first to come. He arrived while Bob was in the hospital, two days after surgery. How different our families were. Bob's family had made plane reservations as soon as they heard the news. No one had asked us if we wanted them to come. They just came. In my family, everyone had asked, "What can we do to help? Let us know if you want us to come." I never asked for help. It seemed like a family rule. I decided that help provided without our having to ask was a good thing.

Ron and I had never had an easy time together. We needed Bob as our buffer. He was our common interest, and that—plus an unspoken agreement to stay out of each other's way— seemed to work. Ron was careful of what he said around me. Racist comments were off-limits. He managed to pull his words back before they totally escaped, as if they were encapsulated in a comic strip balloon and I wouldn't be able to hear them.

It was easier for us not to be at the hospital at the same time. At home, I made it clear that he had to fend for himself. I wasn't cooking gourmet meals these days. As it happened, Ron had developed the odd practice of taking breakfast from home and eating it at a diner with the coffee he ordered. My friend Marsha told him, "Only old people do that, Ron." Ron wasn't so old—fifty-two—but he held on to his pennies with both fists.

Every few days, Ron gave Bob a Hallmark card. Mom sent one, too. This was how they communicated best. Only Roger could say, in his own words, the things that needed to be said about love, dying, sadness, loss. Roger could cry. And crying with us was the best gift he could have given.

We were now battling managed care as well as cancer. Bob had developed an infection in the hospital. He needed intravenous antibiotics around the clock. The insurance company, which was also my employer, insisted on discharge from the hospital. They ordered the nurses to teach me how to put in the IV. I resisted. They insisted. I agreed to have a lesson. When they got to the part about stopping if Bob should suddenly become flushed, signaling danger, I raised my voice. "No, I won't do it. I won't take responsibility for this. I'm not a nurse and I can't do this. I have no training and you can't send him home with me in charge." Stamping my feet, I said, "How can we go through all this surgery, and then you tell me that you are going to put someone who knows nothing about medicine in charge of his health? I just won't do it." Even Ron was impressed. He walked over and put his arm around me. The doctor agreed to keep Bob in the hospital for a few more days and fight the insurance company.

Ron left. Bob came home. Then Roger and Mom came. The family was a tight little unit; not even wives were welcome. It was Mom and her boys. You really can't trust anyone but family.

The mid-April weather was indeed beautiful. We didn't even need to go outside; my in-laws watched The Weather Channel all day. At one point, after the extended forecast, Mom and Roger handed us some pamphlets to read. Buried among them was a cemetery deed. Exquisite timing. "I found this and I remembered you said you wanted it a while ago," Mom said. I didn't remember him ever saying such a thing.

That night, when we were in bed and alone, I brought it up. "What do you think about the cemetery thing?"

"Well, I think it's a good idea. It'll save us some money." The man who never goes to the grocery store without his coupons. If you're going to die, you should at least do it with a coupon.

"But I thought you wanted to be cremated."

"Well, that would be okay, too. But here's a free cemetery plot. Don't you think we should use it?"

I couldn't believe we were even talking about this. Then he asked, "Do you think I'm going to make it?" We didn't say the word death. "This is just in case, right? I think I have a good chance of getting through this. But I've been thinking that it wouldn't hurt to redo my will. Just in case."

"Just in case," I agreed. "You know, I don't remember you ever telling your mom you wanted that cemetery plot. I think it would make her happy, though, if you had it. You know how she is about family and strangers. It would upset her, even if she were dead, to be lying next to a stranger. I still want to be cremated and have my ashes sprinkled in the ocean." I tried to normalize our discussion, as though burial and cremation were far off, only abstract thoughts.

"No, please, you can't do that. I want you there with me." He reached for me. "I need you. You just *have* to be there. I can't be there without you."

I was quite unfamiliar with burial. My family had very little ritual around death. Being scattered to the winds felt right to me, not being planted in the ground. Like seeds, not roots.

"Please, please say you'll be buried with me?" Bob was crying by this time, and so was I.

"Honey, of course. I'll do whatever you want. I don't want to argue about this. Please don't worry. It's okay. I'll be there with you." Who knew where I would be, but it didn't seem so important right then.

FOUR

$\mathcal{T}$he pathologist's report was inconclusive. Perhaps Bob had a ganglioglioma, one of the omas I hadn't read about yet. I hoped beyond hope that it was. He had a shot if it was anything but a glioblastoma. A glioblastoma invades the brain, sinking its ugly fingers deep into the tissue. It grows so fast that there is no way to eradicate it. The median survival rate after diagnosis is one year.

The nurse at the neurosurgeon's office said, "We are going for quality of life, not quantity."

"Well, I want both," I said. I always wanted both. Whenever a stockbroker asked me if I invested for growth or income, I always said, "Both." Why settle?

We got a referral to rehab, where they would teach Bob to compensate for his memory loss. We got a referral to the neuro-oncology department at a well-known hospital in New York, where they confirmed, as I somehow knew they would, the diagnosis: glioblastoma. We got a referral for radiation. We got a referral for chemotherapy.

Bob had called me from the hospital after surgery. "The doctor was here. He told me that I have to have that radiation stuff. What is that supposed to mean? Why do I have to have it? I think they've done enough to me. I'm sick of this!" he had shouted, anger and confusion masking his terror. Radiation was for people who had cancer. We still didn't say the word.

It was then that we knew the thing in his head was malignant. Malignant, malevolent, malicious. How do people talk about this?

How do you talk about cancer and dying, and still believe that you won't die? Will talking about it make it happen? Will it take away that little shred of hope that we hold on to, our belief in the power of belief?

Michael wrote: *In my experience, there seems to be a direct relationship between length of life and quality of medical care. Destiny can't be changed, but there may be many paths to that destiny. You're going to want a second opinion, no?*

I thought about the word *destiny* and remembered an old phrase I had heard at camp as a child. "There is a destiny that makes us brothers," the camp counselor intoned over Sunday night campfires. "None goes his way alone. All that we send into the lives of others comes back into our own." I am amazed that I have remembered this for forty years.

I answered Michael: *I am trying to weigh and measure everything. Right now it seems that speed is more important than seeing more doctors. Radiation has to begin within six weeks of surgery. The problem is, all we have is opinion—I want fact and it doesn't exist. How do you decide whose opinion is best? Marsha tells me that if I don't take Bob to New York, where she thinks the best hospitals are, then I'm not doing the best thing for him. Never mind that he doesn't want to go, and that we are convinced he will get excellent care in New Jersey. It's bad enough to deal with all of this without feeling guilty as well. I think I trust myself to make reasonable decisions, and I believe in Bob's right to self-determination. Beyond that, I can't do anything else.*

Roger and Mom drove us to the hospital in New York. I explained the diagnosis to them as well as I could with as much hope as I could muster up. I read medical books. I read pamphlets from the National Cancer Institute and the Brain Tumor Association. I read books about miracle cures, like Herbert Benson's *Timeless Healing* and Hirshberg and Barash's *Remarkable Recovery*. Of course I read Bernie Siegel. Everyone reads Bernie Siegel, about visualizing the little sword fights between the winning good cells and the vanquished bad cells. I reread *Death Be Not Proud,* amazed at how far brain tumor diagnosis and surgery had come in fifty years, and horrified at how little progress had been made toward a cure. I read everything. Bob read nothing. It wasn't that he didn't want to help himself. He was unable to concentrate. He had started a novel, *Bad Love* by Jonathan Kellerman. He couldn't finish it. He couldn't finish anything anymore, not even dinner.

One bright day, about a week after Bob had been discharged from the hospital, Roger asked me to go outside with him. He pointed up at the trees. "There. See that?"

See what? All I saw were trees and a telephone pole with an electrical box on it.

"Ron made me promise to point this out. He thinks the electrical box may have caused the brain tumor." It's astounding, the lengths we will go to in trying to understand the things that are not understandable.

No one knows what causes brain tumors. Nevertheless, the oncologist had asked for Bob's health history when he was admitted to the hospital.

"Any exposure to chemicals?"

"Well, we live in New Jersey," I answered.

"New Jersey always gets a bad rap. There's no more cancer here than in any other state."

The doctor at the rehab center asked if Bob used a cellular phone. I'd heard this mentioned as a possible cause before, though never by a doctor. Did Bob drink diet soda with aspartame? No more than I did. Did we live under high tension wires?

Bob had his own theory. The brain tumor was retribution for all his sins, specifically for his years of gambling.

And I had my theory, too. The asthma that had been exacerbated by his allergy to our cats had compromised his immune system and allowed a tumor to grow.

We all had our guilts and our blames. The randomness of the universe—some would call it God's will, I suppose—should have been a sufficient explanation.

"And what are you suggesting, Roger?" I asked. "Do you think we should move?" Didn't we have enough to keep us busy right then? And besides, the horse had already escaped. What was the point of locking the barn door?

$\mathcal{W}$e got our second and third opinions. By this time, the man who hated doctors had seen a doctor in Arizona, our primary care physician, an allergist, two neurologists, a neurosurgeon, a neuropsychologist, two oncologists, another neurosurgeon, and the great guru, a neuro-oncologist at the hospital in New York.

Right from the start, Bob had turned over all medical decisions to me. He struggled with even simple decisions, like how much of a tip to leave at a restaurant or what to buy at the supermarket. One day he called me at work to tell me that he had just bought a six-pack of "yellow things" at the store. A six-pack of lemon soda? A six-pack of batteries? What other yellow things came in a six-pack? We laughed when I realized he had bought six bananas.

"I guess with my memory going I won't be able to work anymore. I hope we can live on your salary. I wish I could work. Maybe there's some other job that I could do. But at least I'm going to be alive, even if I'm not as smart as I used to be."

We now had a treatment plan. We started radiation and the first dose of chemotherapy at our local New Jersey hospital. Then there would be monthly appointments with the neuro-oncologist in New York—my concession, I suppose, to those who had made me feel guilty about treatment in New Jersey. The New Jersey oncologist would confer with the neuro-oncologist, the great guru. The great guru demanded that the New Jersey doctor make the first call.

"I spoke with the doctor in New York," the New Jersey doctor said. "He invited me to attend a lecture he was giving this week." It didn't surprise me that the guru was more interested in himself than in Bob's treatment plan. I had believed him when he told us that the MRIs should be read by a neuro-oncologist, not just a regular oncologist who treated all kinds of cancer. I had believed him even though I didn't like him very much. He seemed a little too self-important with his six-page vita on the Internet, and his refusal to acknowledge our waits of two hours or more, and his inability to look up from his computer screen while we sat in his office.

"You know," the New Jersey doctor continued, "we do a really good job at the Cancer Center here. We're proud of the care we give."

I had asked the great guru about Bob's prognosis. "Good," he said. "Your husband is young, in good health, and in excellent physical shape."

Good. To us that meant Bob would get his memory back and live another twenty or thirty years. To the guru, I later decided, it meant that he could probably hold off further deterioration for a while. And to the brain tumor support group that I had found on the Internet, it meant that we had not run out of things to try and that we would beat the median survival time of one year.

We'd been warned that Bob would lose his hair from the radiation. Bob had long, thick reddish hair, which he wore in a ponytail. A friend described him as a Willie Nelson look-alike. Besides the long hair, he had that same scraggly, graying beard. He didn't sing well, though. People often did a double take when they saw us together, particularly people who knew one of us but hadn't yet met the other. Willie Nelson and his conservative, corporate, very proper sidekick. We laughed at how we belied people's expectations.

Bob was never forthcoming about why he had decided on this hairstyle at age fifty. It may have had something to do with taming his flyaway hair, or it may have been because his mother and brothers didn't like it, or it may have been that he was proud of having such a full head of hair at his age. One year he cut off the ponytail and mailed it to Roger, then promptly let it grow again. Now he had cut it off once more, the night before radiation started, and stored it in a plastic bag. A talisman.

Our new life had its own routine. Bob was driving again, now that he had recovered from surgery. I had insisted on a few test drives and could see nothing wrong. It seemed his road rage disorder had been cured by surgery, and his new compassionate self would be an asset behind the wheel.

I went to work every day, and Bob got up around 11:00 A.M. to do some of the chores that he could still do: water the flowers or shop for groceries. Grocery shopping had been one of Bob's hobbies. Everywhere we went we had checked out grocery stores. California to Maine, Mexico to London, and points in between. This was serious comparison shopping. "You spend too much money in the store," he would say. "You don't shop the way I do." Of course he was the better shopper, I agreed, grateful to be saved from the task. Now, however, I begged him to stay out of grocery stores. "Honey, we don't have any more room in the pantry." He would go with a list—paper towels, milk, juice—and come back with salad tongs, Kool Aid, Applejacks, and ten boxes of Kleenex. At least the Kleenex would be useful.

As we spent more and more time at the New Jersey hospital, we began to feel at home. The Cancer Center was quite attractive, decorated in a soothing sea-green with well-upholstered furniture and paneled chestnut doors. The staff moved briskly through the patient list. You almost felt as though you were waiting in an upscale law office, not a place filled with very sick people. In New York there was no waiting room, only a few seats in a hot, dingy hallway, and patients were treated more like welfare recipients than clients in an upscale law office.

One afternoon at the Cancer Center, I thumbed through a copy of *New York Magazine* that profiled the "best doctors in New

York." I saw that the great guru was listed. Before long, the New Jersey oncologist was ready to see us. Bob felt at home with him. The oncologist smiled and laughed, but mostly he listened. I liked him not only because of his warmth and down-to-earth manner, but also because he had a little bit of a stutter. That made him more real. Maybe he was right, maybe we could get good care here.

Bob asked about nutrition. He wasn't overweight, but his diet was not particularly healthy. Lots of meat, few vegetables and fruits, and what he considered to be a daily requirement of chocolate. The doctor said that he would happily add a nutritionist to our growing list of doctors. Eating healthfully was a good idea; it would help Bob get through the ordeal of radiation and chemotherapy.

I consulted with the brain tumor support group on the Internet about what patients were eating and whether vitamins might be helpful. I was thankful that I could find information and support without leaving home. I got to know fellow caregivers online, as well as brain tumor patients and even doctors. It was easy to picture them sitting by their computers, peeling away the layers of daily existence to get at what truly mattered. The group was connected in a way that I had never before experienced. No one in this group was sweating the small stuff.

I noted all the supplements they suggested: shark cartilage, essiac tea, St. John's Wort. There were a million and one things that people swore by. Roger and his wife, Janet, sent us some chaparral tea—if it was good enough for Native Americans, it should be good enough for us—but the smell was so bad we washed it down the sink. After that I bought extra vitamins and some shark cartilage, which I left on the kitchen table. Attracted by the fishy smell, no doubt, Lucky ate the shark cartilage. Our cat, at least, might be cancer free.

Radiation wasn't difficult. I would come home most afternoons to find Bob curled up on the couch with Lucky or our other cat,

Tigey, nestled in the crook of his arm and what was left of his ponytail pulled through the back of his baseball cap. He looked so peaceful I hated to wake him. We would drive to the hospital. Bob would get zapped, as he put it, and we'd drive home.

Bob had been the early riser in our family. Now I was the one getting him up. Staying in bed was a comfort for him. Bed had always been the place of our best conversations. Years before, Bob had joked that my tongue was connected to the light switch. As soon as we turned off the lights, I'd start talking.

"How are things going at work," Bob asked one night. In truth, things weren't going so well. There were rumors about reorganizing and selling the division I was in. Bob knew that I was worried about losing my job. He was more worried than I was. He wanted to be sure that I would be taken care of.

I wrote to Michael: *My life at home is not the same. Everything is scheduled around Bob's medical needs, and I find that I am very lonely because I can't talk to him as I used to. It is more like a parent/child relationship. I imagine that I don't know the half of what loneliness is about yet.*

The next evening, after I got home from work, I cajoled Bob to take the many pills he needed and carefully explained to him what each one was for. "These two are to prevent seizures, these are to keep the swelling down, the Tylenol is in case you have a headache, the yellow ones are because you told the doctor last week that the other ones upset your stomach, this is a multivitamin." Then I wrote down his schedule for the next day, posting it in three different places: "Take pills in first box at 10:00 A.M., in second box at 2:00 P.M., in third box at 6:00 P.M., and in fourth box at 10:00 P.M." Afterward I took his car in for service, filled out his insurance forms, picked up his medication at the drugstore, and cooked dinner.

We ate quietly. I looked at him with his head down, his hair—he hadn't lost it yet—almost drooping onto his plate. He was tired. Chewing slowly, he looked up. There were tears in his eyes.

"I wish you didn't have to go to work every day. I know you have to, but I hate it when you're not home."

"I wish I could stay home, too. Maybe I can ask about taking a leave of absence."

"I don't want you to do that. What if you lose your job?"

I cried then. I couldn't be everywhere at once.

Some days I thought that Bob was ready to die. He had seemed so much better just two weeks earlier. Now he was sleeping all the time and nothing seemed pleasurable anymore. He didn't want to go outside. He shooed the cats away when they crawled up next to him. And he didn't have much to say to me, either.

I needed someone to talk to. It was hard not to be able to share my fears with Bob. I wrote again to Michael: *My jaw ached last night. I realized I had been clenching my teeth for four hours. Bob asked me yesterday if I thought he was going to die. I lied and said, "No, of course not, that's why we're going through all this treatment, so that you will be okay." But I wonder how convincing I was. I have been feeling more hopeless. Every time he has trouble functioning, I worry that the tumor is growing again. I know it would help Bob if I could feel more optimistic, but I can't fake it. He knows me too well, even in his confused state.*

Michael replied: *My jaws ached, too, from clenching my teeth. During the first week after Greg died, I broke two molars. Put on that face that you keep in a jar by the door, Eleanor Rigby. I wish that I had put on a happier face for Greg. Instead, I put on my impenetrable face. That wasn't the right thing to do. In retrospect, death is inevitable for all of us. You'll do better to be honest with yourself and with Bob. Laugh if you can, while you can. You'll feel better about it after he dies—and he will die, either now or later. Just as I will and you will. This all happened so quickly with Bob. Doesn't it feel like you're the first person ever to have to go through this? Of course, in reality you're the ten millionth person to be going through it.*

My friend Kathy called from Florida. She was the type of person who bubbled over with energy and enthusiasm. Bob loved visiting her.

"We're going to be in New Jersey this weekend. We have a lot of people to see and not much time, but we badly want to see you and Bob. Can we come?"

"Of course you can come. We'd love to see you."

When I hung up, Bob just looked at me for a moment. "Nobody thinks I'm going to make it, do they?" he said.

I didn't know what to say. We clung to each other for a long time, neither of us wanting to move, our tear-stained faces as close as they could get.

I wrote to Michael: *I know that Bob is going to die. I think that we are both starting to believe it will be sooner rather than later. It is important for us to acknowledge reality, but we also need to hold on to hope. There's really no answer to any of this, is there? I seem to have misplaced that face that I keep in a jar by the door, so I'm hoping that having visitors this weekend will force us not to dwell on mortality, but will give us a few hours of a semi-normal existence.*

It was becoming hard to remember what a normal existence was. I was drawing Michael into my world of illness. It was like the Bermuda Triangle, sucking in anyone who got too close.

Michael wrote: *I've been more upset over Greg's death in the last month than I have been since he died. I've been trying to think of the reason. Is it the reliving of it through you and Bob? I don't think so. I think that's more helpful for me than anything. Is it my friend and next-door neighbor who is in the hospital on his deathbed? Maybe, but I don't think so. Is it because I realize now that I've lost the love of my life and, like a million other people before me, feel that I'll never find another, even though I might? Probably. Is it because I'm pissed that I couldn't get Greg covered under my health insurance, that he had to go to the VA for treatment, that if he had been insured I'd bet he would still be alive today? Definitely. Is it because I recently became a homeowner and I have nobody to share my home with, not to mention the responsibility and work and expense of maintaining an older home? Is it because I'm tired of sleeping alone? Is it because I'm worried about my own health? Funny, as I said, I just started feeling all this recently.*

Bob, like Michael, was angry at doctors and hospitals. "There is no reason I should be feeling so bad. Why don't these doctors do something?"

"Honey, I know how bad you feel, but even with good doctors there might not be a good outcome." I had never said anything like this before. I wasn't sure why I said it now. Perhaps it was Michael's advice about facing reality.

I wondered if I should ask again about clinical trials. I had mentioned it in the beginning when Bob had just recovered from surgery, after I'd read about some work they were doing at UCLA. "The media tends to hype up these trials," the neurologist said. "There is no cure yet, but someday there will be, and maybe it will be in time for your husband."

I responded to Michael: *I wish that neither you nor I had to suffer like this, watching people we love die. Sometimes it seems preferable just to die myself. The best I have felt recently wasn't when friends told me that I need to take care of myself, but when a friend affirmed how appropriate it was to be depressed—and when she didn't try to get me to do anything about it.*

$\mathscr{A}$t the end of the second week of radiation, Bob invited his former colleagues to play poker at our house. They had visited him
after surgery, and perhaps they knew that his poker games were
numbered. I tried hard to persuade him to skip it this time, but
he wanted badly to have a normal life.

The doorbell rang and Bob answered. The quintessential host,
he had always known who drank what kind of beer. But this time
he couldn't remember. And he couldn't remember his friends'
names, even the ones he'd known for twenty years. Then, when
bringing beer up from the basement, Bob tripped and fell. My
heart ached. I usually had dinner with a friend on poker night, but
this time I dared not leave the house. I wanted to protect him from
falling, from not understanding things, from forgetting people's
names. From brain tumors.

After about an hour of poker, Bob told his friends to play without
him. He couldn't keep the cards straight. He went upstairs to bed.
His friends kept on playing. I wasn't sure if it was out of politeness,
or if there was no such thing as an abbreviated poker game in their
circle. But, for once, there was no mess for me to clean up in the
morning. They had even found the recycling bin for the beer bottles.

Watching Bob become less and less able to function was horrify-
ing. I felt as though I were living with a stranger. One afternoon, as
we headed off to radiation, he looked at me, wild-eyed. "Where are
we going?" he asked. I explained that we were going to the hospital,
just as we did every day, but he didn't recognize the route. "You've

betrayed me. I can't trust you anymore," was all he could say. The doctors thought he should have an immediate CAT scan, followed by an MRI as soon as they could fit him into the schedule. They weren't sure what was going on in the brain. With my help they admitted him to the hospital, which proved to Bob that I was the enemy.

I could do the caretaking, I could talk to the doctors, I could make him take his medication. I thought there was nothing I couldn't do. Except now. I didn't think I could take his fury or his accusations.

Our love had been tested, as married love so often is. When my son Chris was fourteen he had said, "Bob is not going to push me around anymore."

Bob had responded, "And Chris is not going to be allowed to do whatever he wants whenever he wants."

"And I can't let you both hurt each other all the time. It is tearing me up inside."

Then, one day, Chris pushed Bob too far, stealing one of the prized baseball cards that Bob had collected as a teenager. Bob grabbed for Chris's throat. Chris called his father, who called the police.

"I know how angry you are," I told Bob, "but I can't let you hurt my child. He is a child, after all, and you are an adult." Encouraged by Chris and his father, I made plans to sell the house and leave Bob.

A week later, on Mother's Day, I told Chris, "Please mow the lawn. You haven't done any of the things you were supposed to do this week."

"Don't bother me now, Mom, I'm listening to music."

Bob came over and put his arms around me. "I understand," he said, "why you have to do this. But I don't think I can live without you."

In that moment, I knew I couldn't live without him, either. I knew I was making the wrong choice. I told Chris and his father that Bob was staying. "How could you stay with him?" they both raged. Chris decided that he would live with his dad. I cried every night that first year after Chris left. Still, I knew I had not made a mistake.

Bob, much later, was forced to make his own cruel choice. When his employer of twenty-eight years almost went under, he and many others lost their jobs. Bob's response was to develop a full-blown gambling addiction. His life revolved around football, basketball, and baseball, waiting for the next game the way a drug addict waits for the next fix. It wasn't the money. Bob, with all his frugality, had a limit to how much money he was willing to lose. It was his losing that I couldn't take—the dark moods, the self-hatred, his anger at the world, his denial of reality. "I know I can win," he said repeatedly. "I have a system that no one else has."

When he believed he was right about something, it was impossible to dissuade him. Years ago, he had gotten the wrong address for Roger and Janet when they moved to Arizona. After receiving many envelopes addressed to number 81, not 85, Roger called to set him straight. "I can't believe," Bob joked, "that you would build that beautiful house and then move next door."

I packed my suitcase one Monday morning, leaving Bob a note saying that I would be back if, and only if, the gambling stopped. I was sure this was the end of our marriage. I could feel it in every bone in my body. I didn't believe that Bob could give up the gambling. Addictions are powerful. I had pleaded, cajoled, dragged him to therapy, gone to therapy myself. I didn't want to leave, but I couldn't live this way anymore. I stayed away for a week. Bob pleaded with me to come back. And he never gambled again. After that, we knew our bond was so strong that we would choose each other above all else. Till death do us part.

Bob's CAT scan showed a mass on the brain. It could have been from swelling, dying cancer cells, or the tumor. We'd know more once the MRI results were in.

The day after the MRI, I spoke to the Nazi doctor. "What did the test show?"

"It shows that the tumor has regrown."

Although I had been preparing myself for this, I still could hardly believe it. It seemed impossible that this could have happened so fast—two months. I knew that something was wrong, terribly wrong.

"Isn't that incredibly fast for the tumor to have come back?"

"Yes, inordinately fast. I'm shocked, too. But there isn't any question about it."

"He wants to go home."

"Well, now that he's had the MRI, there really is no other reason for him to be in the hospital. I'll sign him out and you can take him home after lunch."

I slowly walked back from the nursing station to tell Bob the good news, that he was able to go home. And the bad news.

We were keeping our families posted, but I wasn't sure how we would handle this. We weren't quite able to let the news sink in ourselves. Bob continued to be so confused that I couldn't tell what got through and what didn't. He knew on some rudimentary level that things weren't right, but he didn't seem to know what it all meant. He certainly didn't want to go back to radiation. Bob blamed the radiation oncologist for his predicament—being back in the hospital—and just that morning had told him to go to hell.

I called Roger to report that the tumor had recurred. After that, I needed to talk to Michael: *The scan shows tumor recurrence. I don't know where we go from here. Bob refuses to go back to the hospital for anything, including radiation. I am so drained that I can hardly think straight.*

Michael responded: *Does Bob's attitude come from his fear and anger about dying, or is it organic? My advice, since it sounds like he's probably terminal anyway: acquiesce to his wishes. There's no sense beating yourselves up over it. All the medical intervention in the world probably won't prolong his life with any quality. What a tough break for you two.*

I was relieved to have Michael affirm that I should go along with Bob's wishes. I couldn't imagine going through more of this torture. If there were a chance that Bob would get well and get his brain function back, I would have gone anywhere and done any-thing. But I knew that nothing was going to make it all right again. I would support Bob in whatever he wanted, even if it meant no more medical treatment. I doubted that his family would agree with this. In this culture, people aren't allowed to choose to die.

Michael added: *As you know, I've been through this. I wonder if Bob will change his mind. Most people choose to fight after they realize that stopping treatment means swift death. It's just human nature. I'd say he will probably swing back the other way and want to start fighting. Of course, this will be after you've made the deci-sion to support him in not medically intervening, and after you've made enemies with his entire family.*

I realized then how fatalistic I must have sounded. Stop treat-ment. Accept the inevitable. I wasn't always this way; the seed of my fatalism had been planted many years before.

"This is the last time we're all going to be together," had been my father's words.

My brother, Bill—that's how he always identified himself to me when he called, as though I wouldn't recognize his voice, or as though I had more than one brother—and I were both married with children of our own, living far from our parents for most of our adult lives. Every family visit ended with Dad's melancholy song, "I guess this is the last time we'll all be together." This was the sadness in a family that valued independence and separate-ness. There could be too much of it. And we had learned to accept it without trying to change it.

Since then I had learned to accept many things, but I still couldn't accept that Bob wanted to stop medical treatment. It was hard to know what Bob truly wanted. I called the great guru in New York. He agreed to see us. Though we were afraid to talk about it directly, we believed that we were at the end of the road. The dead end.

We silently drove across the George Washington Bridge, Bob's MRI scans in a large manila envelope on the backseat. We handed them over to the guru. He put them up around the room, looking at one, then another, comparing them all.

Then, instead of saying, "Yes, the tumor has recurred," he said, "Here's what I think." He addressed Bob. "The tumor recurred before you started radiation, since you started radiation a little later than usual. If you finish radiation and I double your dose of Decadron, I can get you feeling as good as you did when you first came here. We need the full dose of radiation to shrink the tumor, and then we might try the stereotactic radiation, one shot more, to really zap it."

Bob started to cry. The doctor walked across the room and sat down next to him. I was so grateful to discover that he had a human side, I forgave all the long waits for our previous appointments.

"What's the matter? Tell me," he said.

"I thought you were going to tell me that I was going to die."

"I can help you. I'm not promising to cure you. But I can get you feeling as good as you did when you first came to see me."

He didn't say anything about how early it was for the tumor to recur, or about dying. We became instantly less depressed, and Bob seemed less confused and more energetic. The doctor told him he would have to go back to our local hospital for radiation, because no other hospital would pick up treatment in the middle. Bob agreed to go, now that he thought there was some purpose to it. He believed in the power of doctors on this day. The anticipation of feeling better was almost as good as feeling better itself. How the tumor would respond none of us knew, but at least we had a shred of hope. We were riding the crest of the wave again, hoping not to be sucked back down by the wicked undertow. Even if we only got a few semi-good months, I'd take it.

SEVEN

$\mathcal{B}$ob received get-well cards every day, along with food from the neighbors, flower arrangements, fruit baskets, and a stuffed bear with a bandage around his head. And there were the ubiquitous cards from Mom, Ron, and Ron's wife, Jane. Roger and Janet sent us a card with a quote from Annie Dillard, "You can't test courage cautiously." We posted it on the refrigerator. Bob's favorite cards, though, were the construction-paper flowers and the handwritten messages left on our doorstep by the kids in the neighborhood. He missed his chats with the kids. Neither he nor his brothers had any children of their own. Curious. Was it because the need to take care of Mom didn't allow for any additional caretaking? Was it that children were expensive? Was it that the thought of being responsible for someone for their whole life—or yours—was over-whelming? Or was it just circumstance?

The card that touched Bob the most was the one from Tim and his wife, Lisa, telling him to take care of himself and that they were thinking of him. And he cried when a card and a bouquet of flow-ers arrived from Chris. That my children were reaching out meant more to him than anything. And more to me, too. Whether this was for Bob, for me, or for themselves, their reaching out did more than just touch someone—it began a process of emotional healing.

My great hope had been that when Tim and Lisa, and then later Chris and whoever he married, had their own children, Bob would be the doting grandfather. I couldn't imagine it being otherwise. And knowing how one is forever bonded with a person who loves your children, I was sure this would finally repair the stepfamily relationship. It was the belief I had held on to through the dark nights when I mourned my broken-apart family.

Bob and I tried, as often as we could, to do things that gave us the illusion of having a normal life. Our weekend routine of dinner and a movie had to be abbreviated to one or the other. Everything took more time and more energy. Although we pretended to ourselves that our lives were normal, for me, the division between my old life and my new life was becoming more apparent every day.

EIGHT

$\mathcal{I}$t was June now, the month we had chosen for my mother's memorial service. In one of life's odd juxtapositions, my mother had died on that day in February when Bob had experienced those first brain tumor symptoms.

My concern about Bob had forced me to relegate my mother's death to a separate emotional compartment in my brain. We hadn't been able to plan her memorial service until recently. She had been sick for a long time, every year spiraling deeper and deeper into the abyss of Alzheimer's. I needed to bring her back with memories of the person she had once been.

My dad had died five years earlier. At age eighty-nine, he became my mother's full-time caretaker. At the time I didn't realize how hard it was for him. Now I knew what it was like to take care of someone who was so confused and dependent. "She's just not the same woman I married," he would say. Responsibility being the linchpin of our family, the only way my dad could stop taking care of my mom was to die. So, he decided not to have heart surgery, choosing instead to live out whatever time he had left, which was six weeks following his first heart attack.

We had stored his cremated remains in our basement, knowing that sometime in the not-too-distant future my mother's would follow. His ashes sat on the pool table—that way we were sure not to misplace Grandpa. Bob always referred to my family members that way—Grandma and Grandpa, Uncle Bill and Aunt Jackie—

just like my children did. Sometimes he called me Mom, when I wasn't Punky, Baby, or Shuggy.

Since February, Grandma and Grandpa had been hanging out together on the pool table. My colleague Paula and her ten-year-old son, Brandon, visited us in May. On the second day of their visit, Brandon came upstairs from the basement.

"Uh, Gail, I was going to play pool, and it looks like there are two boxes on the pool table. It says on the boxes CREMATED REMAINS. What should I do?"

"Two?" I asked. "Why, there were five last week. I wonder where the others went." He seemed relieved that I could joke about it. We went downstairs together to move Grandma and Grandpa.

I was a little sad to move them from the pool table. It had been easy to talk to them there. I could see why some people kept ashes in an urn on the mantelpiece.

My brother and I had planned a memorial service that we thought our parents would like. We'd decided to sprinkle their ashes in the Charles River, thinking it would please them to be back at Harvard where they had met. Our father had been our mother's lab instructor.

As we prepared for the memorial service, I thought about Michael's neighbor, who had just died. I e-mailed Michael: *I was thinking of you last night. It is awful that so many young and talented people are dying. I hope that you get through your friend's funeral okay. What a sad time, and what awful memories it will bring back for you. As Bob said last night, "Life really sucks sometimes." I guess it's not life, but death, that sucks.*

Michael wrote: *I was thinking of you last evening, too. I feel surrounded by illness and death. This funeral is turning into quite a surreal event. There is the lover and the ex-lover. They don't get along. The current lover didn't want to cremate the body, even though that was what Chuck, the deceased, had wanted. It wasn't until he found out the cost of burial that the lover changed his mind.*

Chuck had cashed out his life insurance in a viatical settlement and built a $20,000 pool in the backyard. He never even got to swim in it. Now the lover wants to scatter the ashes in the pool and then get in and have a pool party. I don't know if I can do that. . . .

I replied: *A first and last swim? I see what you mean about surreal. I don't know if I could do it, either. We are going up to Boston this weekend for my mom's memorial service. I find myself thinking about this as a rehearsal for the next one, which will be far worse for me. I am preparing for the inevitable, I guess.*

The next day Michael wrote: *Let me tell you the odd story from the funeral yesterday. We went to scatter the ashes in Chuck's garden, which is right next door to my house. There were about ten of us. I reached into the urn to grab a handful of what I thought would be powdery ashes, and I pulled out a relatively large piece of tibia or femur or something. I flinched, and the guys all started to laugh. Except for Chuck's terminally grouchy lover, who glared.*

I told Michael: *I'm glad you warned me. Maybe I should take a peek at my parents' ashes before the memorial service this weekend. I'm a little worried about chunks—I think my kids and my nieces might freak out. (Never mind the rest of us.) I envisioned each of us throwing a handful into the Charles River. Now that I know we might get not only a handful but even a few fingers, I will be prepared to dump the whole box. I'm starting to understand why they have laws about where you can sprinkle, if that is the word, these ashes. Who wants to find bones in their garden, or risk dogs digging them up? Do you want to be cremated, knowing this? I guess I still do, but I sure would not like to leave any bones.*

Michael answered: *My friend Bill says if you don't want to leave any bones behind, you have to ask—now get ready for this— to be "double ground." Like a fine cup of espresso from Starbucks. Also, it is sometimes very difficult to get the tops off these urns. They are supposedly sealed for eternity. So maybe you'll want to avoid an embarrassing moment on the banks of the Charles by making sure you can get the tops off without, say, flipping them up into the air twenty feet, or hitting them with a hammer and shattering them into thousands of pieces. By the way, my little dogs seem to show a greater-than-average interest in Chuck's garden next door. I keep shooing them away. And, yes, I still want to be cremated, but I may be the one to start the trend of quadruple-grind.*

NINE

$\mathcal{T}$he memorial service drew the family together from distant places: California, Michigan, Florida, Boston, New York. Bob and I drove from New Jersey. I drove and he navigated, sort of. He was sweet and childlike now, and there was a special poignancy to all of this.

After his surgery Bob had said, "You know, I think it's a good thing that Grandma died this year. I would have had a hard time going to see her when I'm like this." Since my dad's death and throughout my mother's stay in the nursing home, Bob had been my mother's caretaker. He had made it a point to visit her every day, whether I went with him or not.

Bob and my mother had started out in conflict, just as Bob and my kids had. He was a little too rough around the edges, she had said. And she was a little too intellectual and dogmatic, he had said. But over the years they'd found a connection. My mother needed Bob's warmth and nurturance. He was never angered by her growing dependency, as my father had been at times. In some ways, Mom's inability to communicate made her seem fragile. Like a little bird with broken wings. Bob liked to do things for her. And although she couldn't express it in words, she looked forward to his visits. In fact, my brother Bill and I joked that we didn't have to jockey for position anymore. Bob was her favorite.

No matter how rough Bob was around the edges, the softness underneath became apparent in most of his relationships. He had called the police once because our neighbor, Sarah, had let her dogs run on our lawn. Several months later he met Sarah and the dogs on their daily walk. She introduced him to the dogs in a formal sort of way, and they walked back to her house together. They sat in the kitchen for hours discussing pets and stepchildren. Bob usually started with the old football adage, the best defense is a good offense. But it never ended there. A bottomless well of kindness bubbled up when he didn't feel threatened.

The day was just right for a funeral. Overcast, not sunny, not rainy. We were an odd assemblage. Bill, Jackie, Amy, and Sara, the more conventional side of the family, in suits and black dresses. Bob and I, wearing brighter colors. I wore pants, thinking we might have to sit on the riverbank. Tim, Lisa, and Chris, all trying to look formal and respectful in their dark pants, shirts, and ties—not their usual jeans and T-shirts. My cousin Millie. Her husband, Gerry, the only minister in our family of heathens, wearing his clerical collar. And my cousin Lee Lee, who had always been for me the sister I hadn't had.

Bob was tired. He walked slowly, dragging his feet, and he couldn't keep up with the conversation very well. Mostly he just kept his arm tucked in mine. We all took care of him. He took off his baseball cap and showed the kids his half-shaved head and the scar from surgery. He smiled at the solicitude and was happy to stand quietly and be a part of the family gathering. He felt the love and concern more than he understood it.

None of my parents' friends attended the memorial. Most of them were gone now. For my parents' sixtieth anniversary, I had written to the many friends they had collected in their years together, asking them to define my parents' relationship, their friendships, who they were, and what had been important in their lives. I included all of these letters in a memory album. I was glad that my parents had had these letters while they were alive. I believe it's good to know what people think about you, so you can take comfort in it or change it, if you want to, before it is too late.

It was clear from the letters in the album that my mother had been an interesting woman. Each time I saw a picture of Ruth Bader Ginsburg in the *New York Times,* I would think of my mother. She not only had looked like the Supreme Court justice, but she, too, had had a reasoned, balanced approach to life.

When I was twelve years old, my mother and I discussed a book we had both read. She asked what I had thought about the anti-Semitism in the book.

"Your grandparents were Jewish, you know."

I looked at her, shocked. No, I didn't know. Why was she telling me this now? Why did she not tell me before? I thought about this for months—no, years—afterward. The shock and the timing of this information made it seem like a tightly kept secret. I wondered if my mother had a touch of anti-Semitism herself. Was that why she hadn't told me sooner? Or was it of so little importance that she hadn't thought to mention it? Several times I asked her. She brushed it off. For lack of importance or too much importance, I couldn't say.

It was time to begin the service. Gerry read some prayers and biblical passages. Then each of us spoke.

Millie started in her large, robust voice. "My Aunt Diana had her priorities straight. In my own house, the floors had to be spotless. But in her house it was much more important to have seen a ballet or an opera, or to have read the latest novel, or even to have written one." My mother, quietly, without telling a soul, had had her first and only novel published at age seventy.

Lee Lee spoke next. She had a quiet, thoughtful way of presenting things. "Kermit and Diana were always role models for me. They were respectful, independent people who cared for each other, their family, their work, and their community. They once told me, laughing, that they had fought their way through sixty years of marriage. That must have been the element that preserved their independence. Yes, there were always books, laughter, and conversations. But I did often wonder at their lack of interest in material things, and why their house had no curtains."

Jackie was nervous, not used to speaking in front of groups. Her voice quavered as she reminisced about the first dinner she had cooked as their daughter-in-law. "The pot roast stuck to the bottom of the pot with grease everywhere, and the peas were hard and uncooked, but Diana and Kermit ate the whole dinner and said it was delicious."

By now we had formed a circle on the riverbank, standing close to each other like school children about to play Ring Around the Rosie. The road next to the river had been closed to cars. Rollerbladers and bicyclers cruised up and down. Passersby glanced our way, probably not used to seeing groups like this on the riverbank on a Sunday morning.

Amy, my eldest niece, spoke next. She was the newest psychotherapist in a family of psychotherapists, or "psychos," as Bob might have said in the days when he could interject. She reminded us that her career choice was a tribute to the importance that her grandparents had placed on their careers. "And without Grandma," she added, "we would never have learned to write thank-you notes."

Her sister Sara said, "Grandma and Grandpa were always curious about people and willing to listen to views different from their own." I didn't remember it quite that way—my father once stopped speaking to a friend when he discovered that the friend had voted for Nixon. Sara continued, "They quizzed me about school, taught me to set goals for myself and work hard to achieve them."

Tim expressed his gratitude for Grandma and Grandpa's enthusiastic acceptance of Lisa, as well as their support of his chosen careers, teaching and writing. And Chris remembered that his grandparents, though they had high expectations for us all, could accept each of us going our own way. Chris had chosen to pursue goals that were unique in our family: rather than go to college, he was working toward a career as a professional pool player.

Bob held my hand as everyone spoke. He was getting tired, shifting from one foot to the other. I asked if he wanted to sit down, but he said, "No, I'm okay. I want to be here with all of you."

My brother Bill spoke next. "No matter what, our parents' support of us was obvious. I loved them and they loved me. What more is there to say?"

And I? I had treasured our talks over the years, their wisdom, their advice. Sobbing, I ended our reminiscences with a Jewish prayer that I had saved from an Ann Landers column many years before, a tribute to Mom's almost-forgotten Jewish roots.

My children hugged me. I knew that my tears were as much for Bob as they were for my parents. Now I was an orphan. Soon I would be a widow, too. I knew this when Gerry said, "We really should get together again soon and do more things as a family." I knew it when Bob said, in his brief remembrance, "The best tribute to Grandma and Grandpa is this family. What a wonderful family they created. I'm proud to be part of it." And I knew it when I felt my children's comfort. I would need more of that soon, much more. And I knew it when I watched two little ducks paddle up to the riverbank to see what was going on. The souls of my parents had already found other vessels.

Souls. When I was six or seven, my mother and I played a game she had invented: What Color Is the Soul? I didn't know exactly what a soul was, but I liked attributing colors to people. My mother, the color of newly mown hay; my father a friendly black, white, and green glen plaid; and my brother a conservative light blue, the color of a Brooks Brothers shirt, but with red polka dots, like those on a clown costume.

TEN

We had not entirely given up on having a social life. Bob was still the convivial one, flirting with waitresses in restaurants, chatting with salesclerks and people we'd hired to do home repairs. He had always been comfortable talking to just about anyone. It was Bob who became friendly with the neighbors, and even my friends from work had become his friends, too.

In the month of June we had two events scheduled. The first was a going-away dinner for some friends who were moving. I barely remembered how to cook at this point, so our friends brought the dinner. Bob was in good spirits, smiling and listening to the conversation, even joining in at times. My friend Marsha, who had last seen Bob in the hospital after surgery, kept whispering the word "gaslight." When I finally asked what she meant, she said, "Didn't you see the movie *Gaslight?* Bob seems fine. You must be making this up, just the way Charles Boyer did, trying to convince everyone that his wife, Ingrid Bergman, was crazy." Could things really be as bad as I had been telling her?

Our second social event was a block party. The neighbors weren't sure what to say, whether to speak to us or avoid us. One neighbor repeatedly told me, "God doesn't give you more than you can handle." I hated that phrase.

Later I e-mailed my friend Paula, who had visited us the month before: *Remember the neighbor who told me that God doesn't give you more than you can handle? Well, I feel like calling him up and*

telling him that God got me mixed up with someone else. Maybe
someone around here looks like me.

She wrote back: *Mother Teresa, maybe?*

My response: *Yes, I do look quite a lot like her these days.*

She replied: *You don't look like Mother Teresa, but I do think*
you are more like her than unlike her. Don't think that because she
seems pious and saintly all the time that she is perfect. I once met
a group of people who had worked with her, and they said that she
had refused to allow the group to have a refrigerator. Also, some
wonderful soul had gone out to buy hamburgers for the group, and,
being a vegetarian, she had refused to let the workers eat them. So
even saints are not perfect. She struggles just like we do. And I
think she would have genuine compassion for what you are going
through. I can't imagine anyone on this earth not admiring your
courage and strength and persistence. Or is it stubbornness?

I wrote back to Paula: *Stubbornness it is. Like a pit bull. It cer-*
tainly isn't courage. Courage implies fearlessness and choice. I am
doing this with neither. And Mother T. and I are certainly not alike
when it comes to food. I would never limit what people eat.

Especially not what Bob ate. Much to my horror, the one
thing that had always given Bob pleasure now failed to do so. He
had begun to dislike many foods. There were only a few things
that were still palatable. One night we went out for Mexican food,
and Bob had sangria—with the oncologist's blessing. Anything
that enhanced his quality of life was okay, even alcohol. Bob
loved the sangria. But, try as I might to make it at home, it somehow just wasn't the same. The following week he went through a
watermelon phase. All he could eat. We would buy half a watermelon, and the next day I would find that Bob had eaten all the
red part, then neatly stored the crescent of rind in the refrigerator. The week after that was Sedutto Ice Cream week.

I turned to fantasy in order to stay sane. Several years before,
on a trip through Connecticut, we had run across a big rambling

house with turrets and gables and acres and acres of land and a for-sale sign. For a few brief moments we thought about how we might buy it and turn it into a bed-and-breakfast. There was nothing practical about this. We would have to quit our jobs, learn how to attract a clientele, and do all the hard work that goes into running a business twenty-four hours a day. I could do this on my own. Bob could rest upstairs and we could be together.

Or we could move to Hilton Head. This was to be our retirement community. Once we made separate lists of the states where we'd like to live, in order of preference. North and South Carolina were at the top, then Massachusetts, Connecticut, New Jersey, and, inexplicably, Oregon, a state that neither of us had visited.

We would go to Hilton Head this summer, just as we had planned, and start looking for houses to buy, and begin to get ready for our imminent retirement. From the time we had met, Bob had talked about retiring. Every few months he would examine our finances and announce, "We're just one lottery away from retirement." His brothers, although younger than he, had already stopped working full time. I think it had something to do with their dad's death at age fifty-four, the same age that Bob was now. Their dad never had a chance to retire. The sons had to do it before it was too late.

Bob had his fantasies, too. One day he asked me if I'd like to go with him to see the new car he was buying. We went to the lot and he pointed to a little green Geo Metro. "Cute, isn't it? Now that I'm not working anymore, I don't need a big car. I think this will be just perfect for me." It was Saturday and the dealership was closed. "I think we should come back next week and pick it up. I already spoke with the salesman one day when you were at work."

Hollywood, meanwhile, was glamorizing brain tumors. The brain tumor support group on the Internet was, as a unit, furious about the movie *Phenomenon*. Bob and I didn't see it. I doubt that Bob would have been upset by it. Having a brain tumor was becoming less comprehensible, less real than ever. What was real was how he felt on a daily basis, not what was causing the feelings. As for me, I hoped to wake up, find that this was all a bad dream, and live happily ever after.

ELEVEN

*I*n February, when life was still okay, Bob had promised his mom that he would use the airline vouchers we had acquired to pick her up in Arizona and take her to California to see her brother. In Bob's family, as in mine, a promise was a promise. With everything he had forgotten, he had not forgotten this. Besides, he wanted to go. We liked California, even though it hadn't made our list of top five places to live.

Now that the slash, burn, and poison of treatment had been completed, both doctors agreed that another round of chemotherapy would not be necessary—or sufficient. They did not recommend any more treatment. And it was too late for clinical trials; Bob's condition was not good enough. Both the oncologist and the neuro-oncologist encouraged us to go to California, if Bob felt up to it.

There was nothing he wanted more. He willed himself to feel up to it, even though he was now sleeping sixteen hours a day. We began to strategize. I wasn't sure how much vacation time I could take from work. It seemed that the best plan was to enlist the services of the rest of the family. Fortunately, my sister-in-law, Janet, was planning to visit in July.

"I'll take him back to Arizona with me," she said. "Then he and Mom can continue on to California. Maybe Ron can meet them in California and take them back to Albuquerque, since Bob wants to see Ron's new house."

I knew this would be Bob's last trip. It would give him a chance to be with his family. He missed them. And it would give me a respite, allowing me to fit in some business travel. Moreover, Bob's family could experience what I had been experiencing. The cheery cards, "Just get out and get some exercise, man," kept coming, and I needed to convince them that Bob really was deteriorating.

But California was weeks away, and I had put off a business trip for as long as I could. I had to go away for a day. I knew that Bob couldn't be alone, so I asked two of his friends to be with him at lunch and dinner. He was outraged. "Why do you have to get me a baby sitter?" he ranted, like a ten-year-old wanting total independence. "I can stay here by myself."

"Of course you can," I tried to soothe him. "But Johnny wants to see you anyway, and Carol wanted to go out for dinner with you weeks ago. This way you'll have company while I'm gone. And they don't want to have dinner with me. It's you they want to talk to."

"He's furious at you," Carol told me the next week. "He said you don't trust him to take care of himself. Then in the next breath he told me you were an angel sent from heaven to watch over him. You know, I've known him a long time. I think he was waiting his whole life for you. All those other women he hung around with before were just placeholders. It was you that the place was being held for."

Bob and Carol had been friends since the seventies. They had worked together at one time. After that they had co-owned a house together—purely a business arrangement, but one that could never have worked except between real friends. Being co-landlords brought out the true grit of their friendship. They were two of a kind, a little gruff on the outside, direct and outspoken, covering up a capacity for tenderness. Perhaps this is how and why they understood each other. Carol was a single parent. She had decided at age thirty-something that she wanted a child and had conceived Katie by artificial insemination. Bob, had he been female, might have done the same. They made their own choices. Never mind what the rest of the world thought.

TWELVE

*T*houghts of California faded as Bob took another slide down the slippery slope—very, very quickly. It was Fourth of July weekend. Last year we had spent the holiday at a country inn in upstate New York, an early anniversary present from me to him.

"Why did you spend all this money?" he said. "You should have gotten me something practical, like a new vacuum cleaner."

"But we don't need a new vacuum cleaner. I'd rather do something romantic. We always have fun when we go away. Who cares if it's a lot of money? I think it's worth it."

After we arrived at the inn, we walked a few miles along wooded paths, watched a wedding party line up for pictures on the patio, sat by the swimming pool to read. When it began to pour, we went up to our cozy little garret under the eaves to get ready for dinner. And a lovely dinner it was, in spite of the leaky roof and the power outage. Thunder added to the romance of flickering candlelight and a five-course spread. Bob smiled as we attacked our crème brûlée. "You win, baby. This is better than a vacuum cleaner."

We had wonderful vacations, Bob and I. Vacations, we thought, reflected what was going on in a relationship, just the way sex often did. My first husband and I had had dreadful vacations. We had lived in parallel universes. Vacations couldn't make them intersect. But for Bob and me, vacations were as thick and rich and sensuous as the first taste of a milkshake after a diet. Our pleasure, that weekend at the inn, contrasted with the hard work and responsibility in our daily lives. We could never have imagined what was in store for us one year later.

On this Fourth of July, Bob's boss and his wife invited us to a party at their house. It was a cool and rainy day. We dressed in jeans, sweaters, and raincoats. Soon after we arrived, I got a taste of what my social life would be like without Bob. I was used to his taking control, particularly when I didn't know his friends very well. This year we sat in a corner by ourselves, isolated from the rest of the partygoers. Bob was quiet. He couldn't remember his friends' names, or much else about them. To have a conversation you have to remember what was just said. He couldn't.

We tried to eat. I held back tears the entire afternoon. This was the first time I could see how alone we were. In the past, I had had friends or family to talk to. Now there was no one, for him or for me. After an hour or two, I apologized to our hosts, who had tried so hard to help us have a normal holiday, and we headed home.

The next morning Bob could not get out of bed. His whole right side refused to function. It was an effort to walk the few steps to the bathroom. In a panic I called both doctors, but it was a holiday weekend and they weren't available. The covering doctor suggested that I lower the dosage of steroids.

I wrote to Michael two days later: *The guru is playing with the Decadron again. He's sure that it's causing Bob's physical weakness. But I think he's wrong. He says it's too early for the tumor to be growing again. And I believe he's wrong there, too. I took Bob back to the oncologist today. They have hospitalized him and will do another MRI to see what is happening. It will be wonderful if nothing is wrong, but I think the signs are very bad. Since Bob started radiation there's been nothing but problems. The guru says that radiation couldn't have caused these problems. He talks to me as though I'm not very bright. And I guess that's pissing me off, too, but not as much as his telling me that it's way too early for Bob to be decompensating so much. Since when did brain tumors adhere to a schedule?*

Michael: *You are right not to believe the doctor if it doesn't feel right to you. Greg was in a brand-new, state-of-the-art teaching hospital. The doctors changed on the first of every month. His first doctor I called Dr. Happy. Greg was going to be just fine. When he went on a ventilator it was just to "rest his lungs" and he'd be off in a few days. The next doctor I thought of as Dr. Doom. She was always sure that Greg was not going to make it through the night. The truth, of course, as in most situations, was somewhere in between.*

Life was one damn thing after another. I could hardly believe how hopeful I had been in March. I had believed that after surgery we could go on with some semblance of the life we had known, still looking forward to some good times together. Now I pictured Bob in a wheelchair, hardly ever leaving the house. Bob, too, worried about what was in store.

"You know, I really don't see how I am going to get used to being in a wheelchair, but since I have no energy anyway, I guess it's for the best." He would do anything if it meant he could be around a while longer.

In the hospital they put Bob in restraints. He twisted and turned, trying to get out of bed. I felt as if my heart were in restraints as well, twisting, turning, pulling, aching with frustration. "I think they tied me to the bed. How come I can't get up?" Bob complained.

"They're worried that you're going to fall."

I had talked to the nurse. They were worried, too, about his judgment and his mood swings, how he hated the staff one moment and loved them the next.

"Why am I here, by the way?" he asked.

"Don't you remember?" I reminded him. "You have a brain tumor."

His mouth opened and he looked at me blankly. Then he nodded as it began to register. "You know," he said, "I think you might be right."

I existed in a triangle these days, moving between three points: home, the hospital, and my office. They were about fifteen minutes apart. I could drive any of the routes in my sleep. Once, when driving back to my office from the hospital, I heard a song on the radio, "Don't Want to Lose You" by Lionel Ritchie. It became my theme song. I had only to hear the first note and the tears would roll down my cheeks. Hold on, Bob, hold on. I don't want to lose you now.

I went to visit Bob the next morning. "You should have seen what happened last night," he said. "You know that old man in the next bed? Something happened to him and they took him away. There were twenty people in here and then they took him away. It was very loud and I didn't get any sleep." The night before I had heard the man talking to his doctor about surgery. Today, all that the nurses would tell me was that there had been a medical emergency. Bob was right. There had been a lot of people in the room, and it would have been impossible to sleep. Both Bob and I skirted the belief that his roommate was dead. We didn't say the word.

My friend Bess came to visit one morning, bringing Bob a cuddly stuffed cat that looked like our Tigey. It was the perfect gift. Bob missed the cats. And he had always been a stuffed animal lover. When he was a small child, he told me, his bed had been so full of cuddly companions that there had hardly been room for him.

Bob's friend Alex made a hospital visit almost every day. "Ollie," Bob would say, "Good thing we finished painting your house. I don't think I could do it now."

"Oh, you'll be up and about again soon," Alex would say. "We'll find another project to work on together."

Alex's father-in-law had lymphoma, and we sometimes met unexpectedly in the hospital lobby after one crisis or another. I was glad that we had friends through all of this. I was making another discovery. Family is circumscribed by time, place, contingency. Friends are infinite. You can always add more.

It was hard even to pretend to be optimistic. I expected things to get worse. But when Bob asked what I thought, I either lied outright and said, "Absolutely, things will get better," or I equivocated and said, "I certainly hope that things will get better."

I summed it up in another note to Michael: *It continues to amaze me how much people want to hold on to any shred of life. I keep thinking that I would never want to be alive if I couldn't think or couldn't walk, but it may turn out that I will be no different from Bob, Greg, or anyone else fighting for his or her life. I hope I won't be in that position, though, since I don't expect I'll have anyone to take care of me.*

Michael: *That is true about hanging on to every shred of life. It amazes me, too. There must be something that happens toward the end when the reality of death sinks in. I've seen it so many times. People who refused all kinds of medications and treatments want them all of a sudden. Fear of the unknown, I guess. I, too, think I'll die alone. We'll be brave, though. Right? Stalwart, actually.*

I wrote back: *Bob was better last night, able to walk again and a little less confused. The doctor increased the Decadron. Strange drug—he must need a lot of it. He's already on a very high dosage, and he's not having the weight gain, voracious appetite, or other side effects that most patients have. The oncologist said that the MRI does not show tumor growth; it's the swelling and edema that are causing Bob's motor problems. I feel so encouraged. Sometimes I am like your Dr. Doom, always thinking the worst. I'm glad you think I will be stalwart about dying alone. I doubt that I will be. I think I will become an eccentric old lady with lots of cats.*

I brought Bob home once more from the hospital. He was able to walk again with no difficulties. We were glad to have survived another crisis, and life was looking rosier. On the drive

home, we talked about the hospital stay and our relief. Bob
sidled toward me in the front seat of the car. He flashed his cock-
eyed grin and said, "You know, except for the bad parts, it was
okay." Our new philosophy of life.

THIRTEEN

The wind whipped the rain into blinding sheets, knocking down branches from the stately old trees in town. What a day to be traveling. I had a morning dentist appointment, then we were to pick up Janet at the airport. It was difficult to leave Bob alone while I went to the dentist, and I was glad that help was on the way. I drove faster than I should have through what looked like a mini-hurricane in order to get home to Bob and get us both to the airport.

"Roger called," he told me.

"What did he say? No problems, I hope."

"No, no problem. Janet is coming later." I wasn't sure what that meant. Was her plane delayed, or was she coming on a later flight? Bob had no idea. My call to the airline confirmed that her flight was supposed to be coming in a few minutes early. I tried to reach Roger but he hadn't yet made it home, a two-hour drive from the airport.

We dashed off to Newark so we'd be in time for Janet's arrival. But she wasn't among the passengers who disembarked. By now, the wind and rain had turned to sun so bright it was hard to imagine bad weather. Newark airport was getting back to its normal schedule after the delays of the morning.

"Sweetie," I said, "we have to check the board to see what time the next flight comes in. And see which gate to go to."

Bob walked over to the Departures list. "No, that's Departures. We need Arrivals." I had to repeat it several times.

"Phoenix," Bob read.

"No, that's not what we want. We want Arrivals. We need to see what time she's coming from Phoenix. She's not going to Phoenix."

"Here it is. Phoenix." I couldn't draw him away from the Departures list. It was hard to contain my frustration. I felt as though I were trying to explain calculus to an infant. I just wanted to find Janet and get home.

Finally we found the information we were looking for. We had some time before the next flight arrived. I called Roger again. I was leaving messages every fifteen minutes. Then I dragged Bob, who was reading every Departures sign he could find, to the gate.

"Something's wrong," he said. "They always fly on America West. This says Continental."

"It's a shared flight," I explained. "You know how we fly Continental and come in at an America West gate in Phoenix? They do the same here."

"How could this be right?" he kept asking.

I scanned the crowd for Janet, but she wasn't on that plane either. Now I didn't know what to do. I called Mom, thinking she might have talked to Roger.

"Hi, Mom," I said. "We're at the airport. Do you know what flight Janet is supposed to be on today? She wasn't on either of the last two."

She was taken aback. "Didn't Roger call you? When Janet went to check in this morning, they told her that Newark was on hurricane alert. She decided to postpone her flight until Tuesday. Roger said he left a message with Bob."

On the way home from the airport, Bob produced a note. There it was, in his large loopy handwriting: *Janet. Not. Other.*

After we got home, Roger called. "I am so sorry," he said. "I intended to call you back and double-check that you had gotten the message, but Bob seemed to understand. I asked him to get a pen and write it down. I believed him when he said, 'I'm okay, Sammy. I'm getting this down okay. You don't need to worry about me.'"

I was tired and frustrated, but not angry. This had given me a chance to see how Bob managed in an airport. I could see how difficult a trip to California was going to be, even with an escort. Of more immediate concern was how I would manage the next several days without Janet.

Monday came and I went to work. Not without misgivings. Bob usually called when he awakened mid-morning, and this day was no exception. "Hi, Shuggy," he said cheerfully. "What are you doing today?"

"I'm just getting some proposals out and answering phone calls from Friday. What about you? Have you taken your pills yet? You're due in a few minutes."

"Where are they?" It seemed like a normal enough conversation. But after I hung up I realized I probably should go home for lunch and check to see that he had taken the pills. When I got home, he wasn't there.

Two weeks before, we had gone out for dinner. Bob drove. "Honey, be careful," I said with my pulse racing. "You almost side-swiped that car." He realized as well as I did that he couldn't judge the distance between him and the parked car. After that, he was not at all resistant to surrendering the car keys. He added, "I hope I don't go blind. It's bad enough that I'm not very smart anymore. Going blind would be really terrible."

I knew he couldn't have driven anywhere without the car keys. And although he could now walk again, he couldn't walk long distances. Where might he have gone in the twenty minutes since our phone call? After driving around the neighborhood for a few minutes and trying to imagine all the places that he could have walked to, I sat down at the kitchen table, head in hands, tears streaming down my cheeks. The frustration of the last few months, not to mention the panic I was feeling, welled up and spilled over. I went out for another drive around town, trying to assess just how far Bob could walk on his own.

I quickly decided that I would not be able to find him without help. "I'm calling to report a missing person," I told the police. "My husband has a brain tumor and has left the house. He hasn't been gone very long, but he's disoriented and shouldn't be walking around town alone. If you see him, could you bring him home? I don't know what he's wearing, probably a baseball cap. He has long reddish hair, pulled back in a ponytail, and a graying beard. He's about 5'9", 165 pounds. He may not be too happy about being stopped by the police—just to warn you."

A few hours later I sent a note to my friend Marsha: *I had just finished calling the police when Bob walked in. He said he'd just gone to the store for a newspaper. Of course, he was traumatized to think that the police might have been looking for him. He says that he knows he is paranoid, but he doesn't know why. I am learning that when I think he hears me, he really hasn't comprehended or remembered anything. He can't repeat what I say. When I am home I can write things down, but I'm not sure what to do when I speak with him over the phone. I will work on getting supervision for him when Janet leaves. Thank heavens she'll be here tomorrow. I guess he'll sleep well tonight. I guess I'll sleep well in a few years. Of course, I called the neuro-oncologist to ask about his behavior, but he never called me back. What a nightmare. Who could have imagined this? It feels like something out of Kafka.*

Marsha responded: *This is just so horrible for you and Bob. Your worrying seems to be escalating in leaps and bounds. I am not quite sure where you are getting the strength to handle these continuous emergencies. Thank goodness Janet is coming and will be able to help for a little while. I wish I could do something for you when you get so worried. I hope that you will have some respite. It seems that every day brings something new for you to deal with. And I am sure that there is added stress in not knowing what new terrible thing will happen next. Just remember Bob's words, "Except for the bad parts, it is okay."*

Janet arrived the next day. Bob and I were both glad to see her. "I had no idea how bad things were," she said a little later while Bob was dozing. "I'm going to let Roger know how it is here. You know the family doesn't believe how sick he is. Or that he is dying."

It was a relief to hear Janet use the word *dying*. Having someone in Bob's family with whom I could talk openly would make this easier.

"I'm glad you're here. I need your help to convey to them what it's like. Especially with Ron. I called him last week to tell him that I didn't think Bob would be able to go to California. He said, 'I would have gone with him, but it's your responsibility, not mine. You're the wife.' I know how responsible everyone in the family is. Ron would have gone if he'd been asked. But he would have been terrified about having to take care of someone who was so ill, and so unpredictable. I can't say I blame him. But I thought it would help if he could see it himself."

Janet called Roger. "You know Bob is dying." Roger asked how that could be. I got on the phone and reminded him that I had called a month ago to report that the tumor was back. Weren't they going to do chemotherapy? No, they weren't—no more treatment. I repeated everything I had told him the month before. No more treatment because it was too late.

Roger called Ron with the news. Later, Ron told me, "I know you said that the tumor had grown back, but then you said it was all a mistake and the doctor read the MRI wrong."

Where did that come from? "I never said it was a mistake. I wish it had been. Maybe that's what you were wishing, too."

The family began to make plans for another trip to New Jersey. Bob was pleased that they were coming. I was, too. I needed full-time help. Two days after Janet planned to leave, Roger and Mom would come. Then Ron and Jane would follow at the beginning of August. They were coming for a wedding anyway, so they would just come a little earlier. Janet suggested I make an appointment for Mom and Roger to meet with the oncologist. They needed to hear from an authority, not from me, where this was going.

"It's good that Janet is here, isn't it, honey?" I said sleepily when we were in bed. "She can help you get those pills down on schedule tomorrow. And it will be someone to talk to while I'm at work."

"Yeah, it's good. I hate all those pills, though. Especially that Haldol one. Why do I have to take that?" The doctor had decided that giving Bob an antipsychotic might control his agitation and paranoia. It was worth a try.

"It should calm you down so you're not so upset all the time. We just want to make life a little easier for you." I wanted to make life a little easier for me, too.

"I don't want it."

How is it that psychiatric patients always know which medication to reject, which one might change their behavior? I had worked with psychiatric patients during my first social work field placement. Their convoluted thoughts fascinated me. I would manage their lives from nine to five, then go home. Now I was home and I couldn't manage anything.

"I'm not going to take that Haldol," he repeated. Adding as a non sequitur, "You got something in the mail today from Public Service. I don't understand what they are telling you to do. And didn't you say that Social Security was going to put a check in the bank for me? And what about my pension? I just signed those forms. Where is that money going to go?"

Bob was becoming obsessed with money. In his paranoia and obsession were vestiges of old family worries and values. Where would their next meal come from? Never spend a penny more than you have to. Only buy things that are a bargain.

"I added your name to my bank account. Remember? They said we had to have it in a joint account so that I could help you with it."

We had always kept our money separate. Perhaps it was because we had each been through a divorce. More likely it was because we had strong boundaries concerning money. Or maybe it was because my mother once told Lee Lee that "a joint checking account is the work of the devil." We kept track of our expenses and balanced it out at the end of the month. This was the first time we'd had a joint bank account.

The next morning I got up at 6:30 to go to work. I dressed quickly and quietly so I wouldn't disturb Bob. I left Janet a note with the pill schedule and my phone number.

I got to work at 7:30, and at 8:00 the phone rang. It was Janet. She had panic in her voice. "I hate to bother you, but Bob just left. I stood by the door and tried to keep him from leaving, which made him furious. He said he had to go to the bank. Even though I told him that the bank wasn't open yet, he was determined."

"I'll be right home. I have a meeting later. Maybe I can find him and come back in time for the meeting."

I found Janet pacing and looking worried. I knew she thought she had failed in her assignment. "Your neighbor, Suzanne, offered to give him a ride to the bank. Bob took off with her."

"Does she know how crazy he is?"

I waited for them to return. Suzanne's car pulled up to the curb. I knew that she was trying to help. The whole neighborhood had organized a food brigade, bringing us dinners when Bob first came home after surgery. But now Suzanne was almost as agitated as Bob. "He tried to get out of the car while it was moving. I didn't know what to do. He's furious at me for bringing him home without going to the bank."

I looked at Bob. His face was contorted in rage. "I told her to take me to the bank and she wouldn't do it. That's where I'm going. I'm taking all my money out and no one is going to stop me. Fuck you all." He looked like a fire-breathing dragon, snorting and huffing.

"Come on, come with me," I said. "I have the car here. We'll talk about this in a minute." While Bob changed cars, I thanked Suzanne, hoping that my embarrassment wasn't showing.

"Now, what is this about, honey? I'll be happy to take you to the bank when it opens, but you don't have any money in our joint account yet. It will take two months until you start getting disability checks, and you won't get your pension until your fifty-fifth birthday in November." Reasoning with him was ridiculous, as he had no idea what month it was, nor could he understand what I was trying to tell him. All he knew was that no one was to be trusted and we were all stealing his money. The old family mantra: You can't trust anybody.

I drove him to the bank, "fuck you" spewing out of his mouth at every corner. We parked and stood on the sidewalk next to the building. I pointed out the sign that said the bank opened at 9:00 A.M. Then I showed him my watch, which said 8:30. We stood there for fifteen minutes until he got tired. Finally, we moved to the car. "Honey, let's just go home. I really need to get back to work in time for my meeting."

"No. I'm not going home until I get my money out of the bank."

"But you don't have any money in this bank yet. You signed the forms, but right now the only money in this bank is my money."

"I'm taking the money out. So get out of my way." As soon as the doors opened he marched into the bank, fuming, with me following close behind.

I made a quick decision. "How much do you need right now?"

"I'm taking it all."

"Let's wait until they put the money in, then you can take it all. I don't want to close out the account. How about if I cash a check for $200 for today, and we can deal with the rest later."

"Okay."

I handed him the $200, hoping I would see it again, and we drove home.

That afternoon we went to the hospital for a post-radiation checkup. Janet and I were praying that the radiation oncologist would see how hard it was for us to take care of Bob. I asked to speak with the doctor alone for a few minutes, though I knew it would trigger Bob's paranoia. "He's really getting crazy now," I reported. "I don't think I can manage him at home. What about hospitalization?"

But the doctor had been the target of Bob's wrath once before, and he wasn't getting snookered into that again. "No. You take him home. He's okay. Nothing I can do."

Janet and I looked at each other. "I guess we'll go home now," I sighed, hoping that Bob was worn out from his busy day. Not having anything else in mind, we headed for the grocery store. At the store, at least, there was comfort for all of us. Bob seemed happy to pick out what he wanted for dinner, then quickly became petulant again. "Can't you at least let me push the cart?" he demanded. "I'm not a baby, you know."

FOURTEEN

$\mathcal{I}$ lay awake most of the night, thinking about what to do. It was clear that Janet couldn't handle Bob, but I had to go into work the next day. Once again I got to the office at 7:30, and once again the phone rang.

"I don't know whether to laugh or cry," said Janet. "I got up this morning as soon as I heard Bob. I came downstairs to find him sitting in the kitchen sink. His legs were dangling over the edge, and he was just staring out the window. He said he was waiting for you. Then he decided to go out again. I thought I could talk him into staying this time, but no such luck. He looked at me and said, 'Jan, we used to be friends, but that's short getting fast.' He's outside with one of your neighbors now."

"Okay. I just need to make one phone call and then I'll be right home."

This was getting impossible. It was clear that I would have to work a little harder to get Bob admitted to the hospital again.

I raced out the door, bumping into my boss on the way. "I have to leave. I have an emergency. I'll work at home the rest of the day," I told him.

"Just do what you have to do. Things at home are more important right now." Hard to imagine that corporate life could be so humane. Since Bob's surgery I had hardly worked a full day, taking my vacation time in hourly increments. My coworkers and managers did everything they could to make my life easier and give me the flexibility I needed. I apologized for dumping work on others. No one but me seemed upset by it. Still, I found it curious that never once did my boss ask how Bob was. I guessed he was afraid of straying near anything that resembled a feeling.

When I got home, I found Janet outside with our neighbor, Brendan. Apparently, Bob had started walking down the street when he met up with our friend Sarah. Though normally quite persuasive, she couldn't talk him into going back home. No one was sure where he was headed. Perhaps to the bank again. Sarah offered to accompany him. "I don't need anyone going with me," Bob complained. Sarah decided to follow him anyway.

Brendan said, "We can trail them in your car. If you want to move over, I'll drive." Janet, looking worried, went back to the house in case we needed to call her.

There we were, a posse of three, trying to track down the escapee. Bob, debilitated as he was, was able to outdistance us all. No one wanted to make him mad, and none of us dared let him out of sight. It was like being a member of a SWAT team.

As we approached the major thoroughfare, I felt like a mom watching her kindergartner cross the street alone. My heart was having an out-of-body experience. Bob headed for the bank, then stopped in his tracks—workers were fixing the sidewalk along his route. He paused, then marched right into the wet cement. He was dressed in navy-blue shorts, which he always swore were black, and a yellow Bermuda shirt, unbuttoned almost to the waist. His hair hung down, long and disheveled. Now, with his sneakers caked in cement, he looked like a deinstitutionalized patient.

Brendan drove around the block, parked the car, got out, and began walking home. I sat for a minute thinking about how to approach Bob and how I might get him back to the hospital. "Hi, honey. Where are you going now?"

"I don't have to tell you. I'm not going back to that hospital again and I'm not taking any more of that Haldol stuff and no one is going to trap me anymore." The Haldol obviously had not had much effect on the paranoia. Whom the gods would destroy they first make crazy. . . .

"I know you don't want to go to the hospital. We may have to be there this afternoon, though, just to get some blood work done." I had to figure out how to get him hospitalized again. We couldn't take another day of this. "Why don't we just go home now and relax. You had a long walk, and your shoes are kind of a mess. I think we should clean them off." I was trying to appeal to the organized, compulsive part of Bob.

We stood there for a while. Bob did not want to give in. He was never one to defer to authority if he could maneuver around it. At Bob's company picnic many years before, his boss had said to me, "I hear he's calmed down a lot since he met you." I responded, "Kind of makes you wonder what he was like before, doesn't it?"

Now I tried not to be an authority, just a friend, a wife, a lover. Finally he climbed into the backseat of the car, leaving big white footprints on the floor. When we got home he lay down on the couch. While he was out of earshot I called the Cancer Center. The oncologist was on vacation. I told the nurse what had happened and that I just couldn't cope anymore. "Please, couldn't you have the covering doctor see him this afternoon?"

"Bring him in at 2:00," she said. "We'll fit him in between patients."

Relief washed over me as I hung up. Now, how was I going to get him to go to the place he hated most? I let him rest a little longer before gently waking him. "We have to go to the hospital to have blood work done. Don't you remember? I told you we might have to." It wasn't reasonable to try to reason with him, yet I couldn't help myself.

"I'm not going."

"Please? They're just going to do blood work."

"You promise?"

"I promise." I hated myself for lying, but I didn't think I had a choice. I told myself it was for Bob's welfare. Not for mine.

Janet and I got him into the car and tried to chat idly as though nothing at all were wrong. Fifteen minutes later we arrived at the Cancer Center. It seemed a haven in an unfriendly world. To me, not to Bob.

The covering doctor was new to the hospital, young, idealistic, and gracious. He took plenty of time examining Bob and listening to my description of the day's events. He decided to hospitalize Bob to get him stabilized on medication, if nothing else. He made it clear to Bob exactly what he was doing. Bob seemed to respond well, getting calmly into a wheelchair and holding his chart on his lap. We wheeled him through the doors down to the elevator. On the way we passed a McDonald's, the only place for hospital visitors to get food.

"I think I'll have a milkshake," Bob told us.

"Okay. Let's get to where we're going, and then Janet can come back and get you one." I was starting to feel relieved and more comfortable.

When we arrived at the admitting office, Bob got out of the wheelchair. We gave the receptionist our papers, and she called for someone to bring Bob an ID bracelet. It took too long. Bob was eager for his milkshake. I asked Janet to head back to McDonald's, only a few steps down the hall. Meanwhile, the hospital official arrived and put the bracelet on Bob.

Bob took one look at the bracelet and finally understood where we were and what we were doing there. He took off like a marathoner after a gunshot, heading out the front doors and around back to the parking lot. I took off after him. I found him standing by the car.

"I'm not going in there. What are they trying to do to me?"

"Don't you remember that the doctor said they were going to admit you to do a few tests?"

"I'm not going in there. Didn't you hear what I said?"

Janet appeared by the back door. I waved to her, and she headed toward us.

"Janet, I'm having a problem. Do you think you could go back and ask the admitting office to call the doctor and tell him what's happened? I need some help."

Bob paced the parking lot, and I paced after him. He stopped every few minutes and glared at me.

"Don't you remember how nice the doctor was?" Why did I bother to start every sentence with, *Don't you remember?* "He isn't going to do anything to hurt you." I wondered if this was how his mother felt when he was a little kid and she had to track him down to get him to go to the doctor. When we are very sick, do we revert to the behavior of a three-year-old?

Janet returned with the doctor. A nice-looking man, I thought, with curly hair, a plaid shirt, a navy-blue tie, and a cast on his fore-arm from falling off his deck the week before. Focusing on the doctor's appearance seemed like a perfectly reasonable thing to do in the midst of a crisis. It was easier than letting in the fear I felt about Bob.

I was amazed and delighted to see the doctor. I knew I was in over my head. And I knew that doctors didn't usually make house calls, much less parking lot calls.

"Bob, don't you remember when we talked inside, and you agreed that we could do some tests?" The doctor was reasoning with him, too. We human beings don't have many other tools. Reason wasn't working. Force wouldn't work, either. When I pointed to the security guards, the doctor explained that we could-n't force a patient to enter a hospital if he didn't want to go. There was nothing else to do but keep trying to reason with him. The doctor went back to his office and left me to convince Bob that he ought to reconsider. So near, and yet so far.

I watched Bob. Although he looked tired, he seemed to have an unlimited amount of energy. I hoped I could keep up. He sat down on the grass next to the parking lot. I sat next to him.

"You are all a bunch of jerks. I think I'm going to go call Ron. He'll help me." You can't trust anyone but family.

Bob got up and headed out of the parking lot. I tossed Janet my keys and asked her to follow in the car. I trailed along behind Bob for a minute before catching up.

"Okay. If you're going somewhere, I'll walk with you. Where are you off to, by the way?"

"I'm going to that restaurant down the street. I can call from there."

"Why don't we just go back to the pay phone?" I pointed to the hospital.

He looked at me as if to say, *I may be crazy but I'm not stupid.*

We marched along, stopping after a block to rest on a bench. The sky was growing darker, and I wondered if we were in for a summer storm. Getting soaked would be the least of my problems. While we rested, we talked about what Bob was going to tell Ron.

"I'm going to tell him that I am divorcing you. I'm going to find another woman."

I should be so lucky, I thought.

I was going with the flow now, verbal judo, as it were, not challenging or resisting but meeting him where he was. That seemed to work much better than reason. At least he was calm now, less combative. Rested, he set forth again, crossing the street to the sidewalk.

Like a pilot shot down during wartime, I could do nothing but keep us alive until help came. When we reached the restaurant, I would try to call the Cancer Center to report where we were and ask if they could send the police. I didn't know what else to do. As I weighed the pros and cons of this idea, I looked up and saw a black-and-white police car heading toward us. It was as if someone had read my mind.

The police car pulled up next to the curb. Bob looked like a criminal caught in the middle of a bank robbery. I looked like the teller, happy to see my rescuers.

"Can we help you?" There were two policemen in the car.

"Yes. You sure can," said I.

"No, you can't," said Bob.

The cops looked us over. "I understand that you were all set to go into the hospital," one of them said, looking at Bob. "They're waiting for you back there. Do you want a ride?"

"I'm not going there. Forget it."

The cop looked at me. "We can't take him if he doesn't want to go."

"Then what on earth will I do?" I said. "I can't handle this anymore." I was starting to feel slightly nauseated.

"The only way we can take him back to the hospital is if he is a danger to himself or others."

I sighed in relief. "Then give him a mental status exam. There is no question that he is a danger to himself. He can't be allowed to wander around the streets. And I can't prevent him from doing that."

"Okay. What's your name?" the cop asked Bob.

"I know my name, for Christ's sake. You think I don't know my own name?" Bob gave them his name and his address, just for good measure.

"What's the date today?"

"How should I know what the date is today?"

"Do you know who the president of the United States is?"

"No, and I don't care, either. That's beside the point."

"Why don't you just get into the car here. It looks like rain. We can discuss this in the car."

"Why don't you just stop harassing me. I haven't done anything wrong. You can't arrest me. I'm going to make a complaint. Give me your names." The cop who was doing most of the talking took out a piece of paper, wrote down his name, and handed it to Bob.

Bob, borrowing a pen, wrote something on the back of the paper and stuffed it in his pocket. He looked as if he were about to hit the policeman, then he changed his mind. Ordinarily, I'm not in favor of hitting cops, but in this case I thought a pair of handcuffs and a trip in a police car might be just what we needed. At that moment, help, real help, came. There was a clap of thunder and the skies turned black. The rain splashed over us like an ocean wave. Bob, seeking shelter from the rain, climbed into the police car. I got in next to him.

It somehow seemed fitting that for a family that watched The Weather Channel all day, the weather god was the one to respond. Our due, really.

We drove the two blocks to the hospital and pulled up to the emergency room entrance. But now we had another problem: Bob wouldn't get out of the car. Someone from the emergency room came out to speak to him, but he just turned his head away. I sat with him in the backseat for ten minutes, quietly. I reached for his hand. He pulled it away. It felt like 105 degrees, and I thought we would both suffocate. The cops had gotten out of the car and were waiting outside.

"I'm getting out. It's too hot in here. I can't breathe," I told Bob.

He just sat. Then, that instinct to seek shelter, this time from the heat, must have moved him. He got out of the car and walked toward a door that was being held open for him. We could feel the air conditioning and moved toward it as fast as we could. Once Bob made up his mind to move, he kept going. The emergency room staff gave us a room all to ourselves and, having been filled in on the situation by the police, called the mental health crisis team.

They weren't taking any chances this time—a nurse and a security guard were posted outside the room. A padded cell without the padding. Bob was lying on a stretcher. Realizing that he was at the mercy of others, he became agitated again. The nurse, a large, tough-looking man, headed toward him with a hypodermic needle. He held him down and shot him full of Ativan.

"You motherfucker! What the hell are you doing?"

I sat next to Bob, watching and listening. There wasn't anything I could say or do. But at last I felt safe.

In a few minutes he was resting. I moved closer and touched him. "Hi, Shuggy," he mumbled. He handed me the note with the name of the policeman. "Don't lose this, okay?"

I glanced at what he had written: *These 2 maint and obscened at 3 represer two other venues. Ptl gave up on 3 endings.*

It was midnight by the time Janet and I got home. We left Bob resting comfortably, tranquilized to the gills. It seemed as though a lifetime had been packed into a day.

When I got home I checked my e-mail. There was a note from Marsha: *I've called your house several times and there was no answer. I guess you were at the hospital all day. I'm envisioning Bob not cooperating with the hospital staff. But however Bob is behaving, it really isn't Bob. It isn't the guy who refers to you as "baby" and who loves you so much that he cries in the hospital when he sees you. And it isn't the guy who is always so open about his admiration for you that he never puts on any kind of macho act when he's with others. And it isn't the guy who talks about the cats as though they are his children. Or the guy who never hesitates to help out his friends with whatever they need. Or the guy who never really has to pretend about anything. The Bob that you are contending with today has nothing to do with the loving and soft-spoken (maybe not always) guy you married, and I am so sorry about that for you.*

FIFTEEN

The next morning, Saturday, Bob was back to loving me again.

"Hi, baby," he said when I arrived at the hospital. "I missed you. Where've you been?"

"I just went home to sleep. Janet said she'd come by later this afternoon to visit. Has the doctor been here?"

"Yeah. He was here. We had a long talk. He's a good guy."

I turned on the TV for him. TWA flight 800 had mysteriously crashed a few days before, and the news was full of airplane debris, weeping families, and airline officials.

"Aren't Mom and Roger supposed to be coming? I wish they didn't have to fly." I was surprised that he remembered they were visiting. I knew their arrival was important to him. He was afraid they might die in a plane crash and he'd never see them again, never acknowledging that he was dying himself.

The other event on TV was the Olympics. We watched for a while. Bob rolled it around on his tongue, "Olympics, 'Lympic, Limp Dick." He half-smiled. We hadn't made love since the first brain tumor symptoms. "Lovies or sleepies?" he used to ask, pulling me close. Now it was just sleepies, and not even enough of that. It saddened us both. We needed that intimacy more than ever. Sometimes after sex I would cry, not wanting to separate from Bob. That deep connection, that merging of spirit, body, and soul, should not have to be broken.

Each time Bob was in the hospital he invited me into his bed. "Come on in and lie down next to me, Shug. I need holdies." I needed holdies, too. I'd pull the curtain and peek around it to make sure no nurses were lurking. Then Bob would scoot way over to one side and I'd climb in next to him. It felt so illicit, like being a teenager and sneaking around in your parents' house with a boyfriend. A few times the nurses caught us and smiled.

I was glad it was the weekend and I could spend all day at the hospital. Janet and I took turns getting food. Lunch and dinner from McDonald's. Bob was delighted with his daily milkshake. Janet and I dreamed of real food, somewhere, sometime.

The next morning, Sunday, the phone rang at 6:00. I lunged for it, fearing something awful. "Hi, Shuggy, I think I've been in an accident. There's blood all over my hat. I might be in the hospital. Can you come visit? The name of the hospital is St. Something or other. I think you might know the way but just in case you don't, remember to make a left at the restaurant. Okay?"

"I'll be there as soon as I can. It's 6:00 A.M., so it will take me a little time. I'll try to be there by 7:30." I didn't take him seriously about the accident—he was so confused about everything—and I knew where he had been all night. Besides, I needed a little time by myself, and a breakfast that wasn't from McDonald's.

When I got there, Bob was sitting up in bed with his hat on, blood all over it. I went to get the nurse. "What on earth happened?"

"Everything's okay. He pulled the IV out by mistake when he tried to get up to go to the bathroom. It was kind of a mess. But he's fine."

The next morning, Janet woke up with a stomach virus, or the consequences of too much fast food. Marsha came with me to the hospital after work. We went out for dinner after that. This was the first time I had gone out with a friend in months.

"When do you give up hope?" I asked.

"Never," she said. Her husband had died of cancer when she was twenty-nine years old, leaving her to raise three small children alone. "You believe until the very end that there will be a miracle and your husband will not die."

"Thanks for going through this with me. You don't know how much I need to talk to you every day." I looked up and saw tears in her eyes. It surprised me. She took great pride in never crying about anything. The worst had happened years ago. Every other crisis paled in comparison.

"It's an honor," she said. Now we both had tears.

The waiter took one look at us and decided to return later.

"He probably went back to the kitchen," I said, "and told his friends, 'I don't know what's wrong with them; I just told them the specials.'"

SIXTEEN

The next day was July 23, our twelfth wedding anniversary. Bob and I had happily celebrated every occasion but St. Swithin's Day. Had we known when it was, we would probably have celebrated that as well. This year, though, Easter, Mother's Day, Father's Day, Memorial Day, and Independence Day all passed unmarked by cards, gifts, or celebratory dinners. I wanted to find Bob an anniversary gift, but I couldn't think of anything. It was not within my power to give him the gift of a longer life, the only gift that would have mattered. I wrote him a note telling him how much I loved him and how glad I was to be married to him, and I brought a strawberry milkshake and chocolates for good measure. Bob didn't know it was our anniversary. He read the note and promptly forgot about it.

Janet said her goodbyes to Bob before I drove her to the airport. He gave her a big hug and kiss and told her she was a real friend. He cheerfully waved goodbye, sitting up in his hospital bed, wearing the Sedona hat that Mom had given him after surgery. "That's the classiest hat I've ever had," he had proclaimed when he opened the package.

Janet and I wept all the way to the airport. "What will you do when he dies?" she asked. "Can you move out to Arizona near us?" We both knew that she would never see Bob again. Roger was coming now, and Janet needed to go home to their sick dog. Their dogs were their children, just as the cats were ours.

Mom and Roger came a few days later. The oncologist had suggested that we begin looking for a nursing home with a hospice function. I had heard the old joke about being nice to your daughter-in-law, as she'll be the one to choose your nursing home. But it isn't funny at all when your daughter-in-law is the one choosing your son's nursing home.

We looked at two.

"The people here are so old and sick, how's he going to fit in?" Mom asked.

"It's depressing me, too, Mom. But we don't really have a choice. I can't take care of him at home, no matter how much help I have. It was terrible when I had to put my mother in a nursing home. This is even worse."

The second nursing home we looked at was a little better. We spoke with the insurance company to arrange transportation for him the next day. That afternoon, Mom, Roger, and I conferred with the oncologist.

"Could you talk to us about what to expect next?" I asked.

"Bob is very sick," he said. "I wish I could tell you otherwise."

"Doctor," Roger asked, "how much longer do you think he's going to live?"

"Not much. It could be a few weeks or a month. He will possibly get even more confused than he is now. Then his systems will begin to shut down. You may be able to take him home at that point, but for now I am recommending the nursing home, just because he's so unmanageable."

"I have another question." Roger looked at the doctor. "I guess this is somewhat self-centered of me, but I have to ask it anyway. My dad died of a heart attack at age fifty-four, now my brother is dying of cancer at age fifty-four. Do I have to worry about dying at fifty-four?"

"I'd be more concerned about heart disease than a brain tumor," replied the doctor, as he surveyed the somber family sitting across from him. "I am so sorry." He addressed me now. "Bob is such a nice person. And you are, too. I wish this hadn't happened to you."

I thanked him for meeting with us. He put his arm around me for a minute. I wouldn't be seeing him anymore now that Bob was being discharged from the hospital. That saddened me. He had treated us as a couple facing fear and uncertainty, not as just another cancer case. I wasn't surprised when he told me that his mother was a psychiatrist.

We left the Cancer Center and went upstairs to Bob's room. Mom stayed with Bob while Roger and I walked down the hall to get them some juice.

"How is Mom dealing with all of this?" I asked.

"She's doing okay. But she's concerned about you. She knows what it feels like to have a husband die."

The tears came then. We held each other, sobbing. "You're a wonderful woman," Roger told me. "If you meet someone in six months and want to get married again, go ahead and do it."

I just shook my head. The thought was totally beyond my comprehension. But I loved that Roger was giving me permission to take care of myself in any way that I wanted or needed to. It was especially meaningful in a family that had such strict rules about the right way to do things.

$\mathcal{B}$ob seemed delighted to leave the hospital. He waved from the stretcher as he was being loaded into the ambulance, chatting with the doctor, not even asking where he was going. He seemed to think the ride would be fun. I could only hope that the nursing home, too, would seem more like an adventure than an incarceration.

Roger, Mom, and I followed behind. "I guess this is a good thing." My tone suggested that I wasn't entirely convinced. "I know he can't stay in the hospital any longer. I wish he could come home."

The nursing home gave Bob a twenty-four-hour sitter, a Haitian man who simply sat and watched us. It made us uncomfortable. Bob couldn't understand plain English now, much less English with a Haitian accent; the sitter might as well have been speaking Farsi. Mom said, "How do we know this guy is trustworthy? They're all lazy, you know." It wasn't going to be a good day.

I went home to get clothes for Bob. The nursing home didn't want him in bed all day. He should be up and about, being rehabilitated. Rehabilitation for what, for Christ's sake? For the last two weeks of his life? Maybe Ron had been talking to them: "Just make him get out and get some exercise, man. He'll be fine."

Bob was not in bad spirits. He seemed happy to have Mom and Roger there. And Ron and Jane would be coming soon. He no longer worried that they were coming to visit because they thought he was going to die. He just tried to make sense of what was going on each day.

"Last night that big purple thing was here," he told me after his first night in the nursing home. I was unfamiliar with the nursing home routine and had no way of knowing what purple thing he might be referring to. We began our usual question-and-answer routine.

"What kind of purple thing?"

"You know. That dragon."

"A purple dragon?"

"Yup. It was right over there in the corner. Singing."

"Do you mean Barney?" I didn't think he knew about Barney. Maybe one of our friends with small children had mentioned him.

Bob was walking quite well again, now that he was no longer hooked up to an IV. The sitter walked him all over the nursing home. Going outside was risky, though. On this day he followed me out to the parking lot and tried to climb into the car.

"Aren't we going home now?"

"Not tonight. In a few days, maybe." I hoped that this was true. I never knew anymore if what I was telling him was the truth or a wish.

"Well, I want to go home with you now."

"Let me walk you back to the room. We'll talk about it." Perhaps Bob was sensing my discomfort. I hated the nursing home. The hospital was like a second home. This wasn't. Here I felt queasy and anxious. Why was it so different from the hospital? Had I told myself that hospitals are where people get well and nursing homes are where people die?

I managed to get Bob settled in bed with the television on and the sitter sitting. Mom, Roger, and I went out for dinner.

"This restaurant must not be any good. There's no one here," Mom complained.

A few minutes later the room started to fill up. Soon the tables closest to us were occupied. Mom picked up her glass of wine. "Why do they have to seat people so close to us?"

What did it matter? Bob was dying.

The next day, Ron and Jane arrived. It was Jane's birthday. Family tradition had it that birthdays were to be celebrated with restaurant dinners and lavish gifts. I hadn't been in a store in months. I couldn't even remember what it was like to shop for a gift. So I had bought Jane a balloon and a cookie from the convenience store at work. That was all I could find.

I hurried from work to the nursing home so I could see Bob before Roger brought Ron and Jane over. I didn't know if Bob would remember that they were coming. It would be easier if I got there first, paving the way for the visit. This way I could assess Bob's state of mind before the rest of the family arrived, so I'd know if I needed to act as a buffer or an interpreter.

"Where's the big guy?" Bob asked. He did remember they were coming; he just didn't remember Ron's name.

I wondered how Ron would react to the nursing home. This wasn't easy for any of us. But Ron seemed as glad to see Bob as Bob was to see him. If he was upset about the nursing home, he hid it well from all of us. I was pleased that Ron was cheerful and that my own feelings weren't coloring the visit.

Later that night I wrote to Michael: *Things are pretty tense. After all those years with my mother in a nursing home, I can hardly stand to have Bob there. Some days I long to get this over with, but then I feel guilty and sad because, as you told me not long ago, I know that I will wish he were still here, even in such unstable condition. And I will miss him terribly. He badly wants to be at home, and now he seems weak enough that we may not have difficulty controlling him. I want to make this a peaceful, loving death if I can. Roger and I cry together every night. It's good for me to have him here.*

Michael replied: *This is just heartbreaking. Yes, I think it would be better to have him home if it is possible, mainly because that's where he wants to be. It amazes me that your actions and reactions are all so appropriate. Are you as well-composed on the inside? I remember just operating in a blur at the end. There were times when I would arrive at the hospital feeling sure that I'd find an empty room and Greg would already be in the morgue. I remember how close to breaking I felt, like there was electricity, not blood, flowing through me. Shock, I guess. I wish you and Bob could have had longer together, but since death appears to be inevitable, I'm glad it's going to be relatively quick. Greg was very sick for fifteen years.*

EIGHTEEN

$\mathcal{S}$o we took Bob home to die. And he did not go gentle into that good night.

The caravan of two cars—Bob and I and Roger in one; Mom, Ron, and Jane in the other—pulled into the driveway. Bob had been away for almost three weeks, probably the longest he'd ever been away from home at any time in his life. We were all excited about the homecoming, as if I were a mom arriving with her newborn. Did the return home, in some way, symbolize getting well, or did it just represent the comfort of familiar surroundings?

We loved our house, though we'd never expected to buy it. It had been advertised in the local paper one week and we decided, just for a lark, to take a look. I was sold the moment I saw the built-in bookshelves in every room. For Bob, the big trees in the backyard, the slate roof, and the chestnut woodwork did it. From then on, Bob became a committed decorator. After work and on weekends he'd just pick up a paintbrush. It seemed to relax him, finding new places to work on: the basement floor, the bathrooms, the garage, even the closet where we stored the paint. Nothing went untouched. He'd show his handiwork to anyone who would look. But now, the house, like everything else in our lives, didn't quite feel or look the same.

The social worker and the nurse from hospice came to the house to meet with us. They had ordered a hospital bed, which we set up in the den on the first floor. Bob wasn't enthusiastic about visitors; being home again seemed to trigger his paranoia. Even his brothers couldn't calm him. While I was at work for a few hours, Bob, for reasons that no one could fathom, chased Roger around the house. Roger escaped, but Bob headed to the garage where the tools were stored. He needed a weapon, he said. Since Roger was wisely keeping his distance, Ron was left to calm Bob. But it was Jane who finally talked him into returning to the house—without the ax he held in his hand. Neither she nor anyone else could identify the source of his anger.

The afternoon passed slowly. "Let's not make up the hospital bed yet. I think it would be nice for him to sleep in his own bed tonight. With you," Roger said.

I wanted that, too. I didn't know how many more nights we would have in the same bed. Bob ate dinner voraciously: chicken, fresh Jersey corn and tomatoes from the local farm stand, and ice cream. He ate with gusto, food being a pleasure once again. We encouraged him, urged him to eat more. It felt as though things had stabilized. Bob home, surrounded by family, the firestorm extinguished. We all talked, shared chores, picked up the pieces. What could be wrong? It felt like one of the many family get-togethers we had had over the years.

That evening, Bob climbed the stairs slowly, very slowly. Every step was an effort. I was glad we had put the hospital bed downstairs. We got to our room and he collapsed on the bed. I helped him put on the pajamas I had bought for his nursing home stay. As long as I'd known him, he'd never owned a pair of pajamas. We crawled into bed.

"Lovies or sleepies?" he grinned.

"I guess it's sleepies; it's been a long day. I think we're both too tired." The journey up the stairs had been like our journey through the last five months—full of reluctance, sorrow, pain, and exhaustion. Just remembering life as it had been, our real life together, helped me. We held hands and drifted off to sleep.

The next morning was Sunday. Bob got up around 8:00. He was disoriented and groggy. I walked him to the bathroom. He stood next to the bathtub, looked at me, and said in a low voice, "I just can't do this anymore." That was all he said.

He refused to take his pills. No amount of urging made a difference. He wanted nothing to drink or eat. I called hospice.

"Don't force anything on him," the nurse said. "He's in charge now. And he's telling you what he needs. His body does not want food or water. Soon it will begin to shut down."

I walked Bob down the stairs. He didn't say anything, but he was happy to climb into the hospital bed. The hospice nurse came and checked his vital signs. Then she talked to Roger and me. Mom didn't like to get involved with medical concerns, and Ron was in the garage, isolating himself from the craziness, or perhaps even more from the sadness.

"When patients are dying," the nurse told us, "even though it appears they are comatose, they can still hear. Hearing is the last thing to go. Tell him what you want him to know. He'll hear you. And tell him, if you want to, that it is okay for him to let go."

Bob was sleeping now, tossing and turning. Mom worried that he would have pain. The nurse said she would order morphine. There isn't a lot of pain with brain cancer. They could make sure he was comfortable.

Mom covered him with a blanket. It was August, but the air conditioner was on. And, besides, it is a mother's role to cover her child with a blanket. I rubbed his feet and his back, but he pushed me away. Mom had held his hands in the nursing home the week before. "Mom's hands are five percent softer than yours," he had said to me. He still liked to quantify things, the way he had every fall when he counted the bags of leaves he had raked, or every winter when he counted the shovelsful of snow he had removed from the driveway, or every summer when he reported how many roses he had deadheaded from the bush.

I whispered, "I love you, honey. You'll be in my heart forever." He held my hand now; he wasn't talking anymore. Mom and Roger sat in the room with us. The TV droned in the background. They were watching the Yankees and the Mets today, not The Weather Channel. I went to the door to let the home health aide in. She would bathe Bob and change the Depends. His systems were shutting down quickly.

Ron came in from the garage. "The nurse says that Bob will mostly sleep now. And we will just keep him comfortable," I told him. "She says he can still hear."

"Don't worry," Ron said. "I won't say anything bad about him."

NINETEEN

The week was a blur. I was not going to the office at all anymore. My friend Marsha came to say goodbye to Bob. She brought flowers. We stood by his bed in the den. "Is this like sitting shiva in advance?" I asked.

"Yes. I think so. Except someone else would be answering the door for you, and people would bring food, not flowers."

My brother called. "What can I do to help you? I'm going to be in New York for a few days."

"I think I could use a hug. Why don't you come if you can."

Bill and I went out for lunch, just the two of us. "Where will you go? What will you do?" he asked.

"I'm staying right here. No changes. I have my job. I want to keep the house."

"Would you like to come visit us for a while?"

"I don't really have any vacation time left. It doesn't matter. I don't have anyone to go on vacation with anymore."

"You'll have someone. Maybe not someone with a ponytail. There will be vacations again."

Our neighbor, Beth, brought us brownies. When she left Mom said, "I can't believe that someone in this neighborhood can't dress better than that. That blouse must be fifteen years old. And those sneakers. Did you see how dirty they were?"

"Mom," Roger said, "she's been gardening. And she's doing something nice for us. Can't you lay off the criticism for a little while?"

Tim and Lisa phoned from California. Chris called from New York. "What can we do? How can we help?"

"Will you come to the funeral? I think it will be soon."

Bob's boss called. "Can we come? Can we bring Travis? We told him that Bob is very sick. He wants to see him. Bob has been so good to him. We know he's only six, but we think it's okay if he sees someone who is dying."

Ron was horrified. A six-year-old and a dying man. It is a shame. Dying is a private matter, not for observation, especially not by children. Ron was doing the grocery shopping now, and taking the cars for service, and trimming the trees, and cleaning the garage—his place of refuge. He only came into the house to eat and watch baseball on TV. Jane was no longer there. She had gone to south Jersey for a wedding and to visit her mother.

Roger's friend Lori came several times. She had just finished nursing school. She held Bob's hand and touched his cheek with great tenderness. She wanted to work in a nursing home, she said. Roger and Janet's dogs were born at her house. Her mother was the breeder. Did this make her a relative?

At night, Roger and I talked about Bob, reviewing his life and loves. Women liked Bob because Bob liked women. Once I asked Bob where he had learned to treat women so well. He said he'd watched his dad.

Roger told me what it was like when their father died so suddenly. He had been fifteen, Bob twenty-four. He told me how alone he'd felt, how he'd had no one to talk to. How he would drift away from people, unanchored, as if he were floating in space, no ground beneath him.

We watched Bob. Roger said, "This will sound funny, I know, but this is one of the best weeks of my life."

"It is really a spiritual experience, isn't it?" I answered. "Being with someone you love in his last days on earth." It was also, for Roger, a way to grieve his father's death so long ago.

We were giving Bob morphine every six hours now. He fought me when I tried to open his mouth to put the dropper in. "You bitch," he said once. I turned to Roger, "Are those his last words to me? How romantic." His respiration had slowed and become rheumy. The nurse ordered scopolamine to dry up the phlegm. I thought I remembered a murder story where scopolamine was the lethal drug given. I slept on the couch in the den next to Bob. Roger slept on the couch in the sunroom in case I needed help. Ron and Mom were upstairs.

We were walking slowly, calmly, peacefully, inexorably through the Valley of the Shadow of Death. I got another e-mail from Michael:

I had a dream last night that you and I and Bob built a concrete porch behind my deck—I don't even know what Bob looks like, but there he was in my dream. A fine porch it was, too—strong, sturdy, and perfect. I think I told you before that I believe in reincarnation. I believe that the people you feel strongly about, like Bob, are a part of you forever. And you will never be away from them, not in the long run. I love you, Gail.

A week had passed. My friend Meredith came to visit from San Antonio. We didn't see each other often. We walked for miles. It felt good; I didn't leave the house much anymore. Our children were the same age and had grown up on the same block. Meredith and I had gotten divorced from our first husbands the same week. And now the deaths of people we loved touched us both—her daughter had been murdered less than a year before.

The nurse told us that Bob was near the end of his struggle. His hands began to turn a mottled blue. His breathing was raspy and irregular. It would not be long now. "It's okay," I whispered to him. "You can go when you're ready. I'll be here for now. I'm glad we found each other. We were so lucky. I'll never forget you. I'll never stop loving you. Peace, my darling."

And so Bob died. Some deaths blaze like the dying leaves in the fall, and some roar like the waves that end on the sand. Bob's was quiet and melting. It was 8:00 on a Monday morning. Hospice had told us that some patients wait until their family members are out of the room before they die. But I knew that Bob would die with me by his side. I got up from the couch and stood next to him. His breathing was slow and irregular. A breath, then a long silence. There were three breaths like that. I put my hand on his cheek. There was one last breath, and then he was gone.

I stood beside him for an eternity, it seemed. Just thinking. Wondering where he was now. How could it be that someone can be here one minute and not be here the next? I went to get Roger. "He's gone," I said. "It's over." Roger, too, stood reverently for a minute by Bob's bed. Then he slid Bob's wedding ring from his finger and handed it to me. He slowly and gently folded Bob's hands across his chest, then went to wake Mom and Ron. I called hospice.

PART TWO

TWENTY

It was day one. There were three hundred and sixty-four left. The books tell you that you will mourn for a year when a loved one dies. You shouldn't make any big changes in your life during that year. But how does anyone know how long it will take? Grief is like a fingerprint, the whorls and patterns a little different for everyone. I was at the beginning of grief. I knew that. You do not start to mourn, in a real way, until day one.

The week was a collage of activity: flowers, food, a church, music, airplane reservations. Jane came back from the Jersey shore and gave Ron a Hallmark sympathy card. Janet arranged for a dog sitter so she could be here for the funeral. I took Xanax so that I could sleep.

The family gathered once more. It was the last time that my family and Bob's would be together. The link was lost, the chain broken. Gerry, my cousin's husband, was officiating, as he had for my mother and father. "The real minister is on vacation," Mom had told us after calling her church. The church that Bob hadn't attended since he'd gone to Sunday school a hundred years before.

I took charge of the arrangements. Roger and I picked a hymn. He suggested the Cat Stevens song, "Morning Has Broken." I was impressed that he knew it was a hymn before it was a Cat Stevens song. Bob would have liked that, a non-hymn hymn. The real hymns would be on vacation along with the real minister.

I was on automatic pilot. The only important thing I had to do was work on my eulogy for the memorial service. I didn't think of it as a eulogy, really. Reflection was a better word to describe it. I asked Ron and Roger if they would speak, too. Janet wanted to say something as well. And Bob's friend Carol. Later, Chris said, "I wanted to say how much it meant to me that Bob took such good care of you and loved you so much." He didn't say anything at the funeral, though. He had always been afraid, he said, of Bob's family. At the beginning of our marriage, my friend Kathy had said, "How good it is for Tim and Chris to see how Bob treats you. Of course, Bob probably won't be calling you 'my wonderful baby' forever." Not forever. Just for the rest of his life.

It was not hard to tell the church full of mourners what our marriage had been, what this man had meant to me. It would have been harder not to tell them. Ron was the only speaker who cried. I was astounded.

The memorial service was over, but the dense fog of that first week continued. It was still hard to focus. I felt as if I were viewing the world through a translucent glass, able to see shapes and colors but nothing more. My family left. Then Bob's. I went back to work. But life would never be the same.

I sent a posting to the brain tumor support group to let them know of Bob's death. I didn't want to drop out of the group yet. There were many people whose stories I still followed, like characters in a novel that I didn't want to put down. Reading their stories and struggles helped to fill the emptiness in my life. And in some way, it was a connection to Bob. There were odd little things like that—staying in the brain tumor support group, driving by the Cancer Center, listening to his voice on the answering machine. All of those things brought him back to me, comforted me.

I had yearned, when Bob was so sick, to be near the water. The peace that I longed for in the deepest center of my being was there.

I wanted to go to the ocean and listen to the waves beat upon the sand, to be hypnotized by their rhythm and constancy. Finally, one Saturday, I went. I spread my towel a few feet from the ocean's edge. As I gazed at the gray water, I thought of the picture on my bedroom wall: trees at the end of autumn, dots of scarlet and orange, muted grays and blues. At the bottom a quotation by Euripides: *There is something in the pang of change, more than the heart can bear. Unhappiness remembering happiness.* That's where I was now. Being alone was the new order of things. I would let the solitude and the waves heal me.

As I had left the house, I caught a fleeting glimpse in the mirror that made me wonder about the person I saw. A short woman, blonde by nurture, not nature, always struggling to get her weight lower than her IQ and thinking it would be easier just to get smarter. A woman of the age that they were now calling "not-yet-ready for Medicare," near elderly. Who was she now? Still a mother, still a social worker, still a corporate manager, a sister, a friend. But not a wife.

What is this role of widow? How do you start? Does it start when that form first hits you and you have to check off single, married, or widowed? Does it start when you come home from work the first week after your husband dies, call his name, and realize no one will answer? Does it start when you take your husband's name off your homeowners' insurance policy? For me it started when I joined the hospice bereavement group. I had an identity there. There were other people like me. I didn't feel so isolated and so different.

Most of us were widows or widowers, though a few had lost parents, or siblings, or even children. And most of us had watched our family members die of cancer. It was a disparate group: all ages, all colors, all ethnicities, all socioeconomic levels. That made it richer. We would learn that the emotions of death were similar, no matter what our differences were.

Michael and I were corresponding quite regularly now. I wrote: *I'm glad to be back at work. Since the funeral, and since my in-laws left, I have been free to feel the pain. And it's there—big time. I'm going to therapy and joining a bereavement group. After all these years of recommending support systems to others, it's time to take my own advice. My mother-in-law is a good example of how not to grieve. Bob used to say that she had never forgiven his father for dying. I don't want to be like that.*

Michael answered: *You are priceless. People we don't want to be like are sometimes more influential than people we do want to be like, don't you think? It's not often that I say to myself, "Boy, I'd really like to be like him." More frequently it's, "If I'm ever like him, just take a gun and put me out of my misery." After Greg died, I felt very close to people who really seemed to understand and acknowledge my pain. If you need to get away for a while, come stay with me. I have a nice spare bedroom, if you don't mind sharing with raccoons.*

TWENTY-ONE

One day on our lunch hour, Marsha and I went for a long walk, winding our way through the curving, shaded streets of suburbia, passing long, sloping lawns and regal houses. She stopped to remove a piece of gravel from her shoe.

"So," she asked, "what will you do now? Will you move, change jobs? What will you do?" Odd how people seem to expect you to change something when a spouse dies, as though there haven't been enough changes in your life. They haven't read the widow books.

"I'll go where life takes me," I said.

The year before Bob's brain tumor had been diagnosed, a friend's husband was murdered in a post office robbery. After that, she committed herself to working ceaselessly to get guns off the street. No one else should have to suffer such a senseless loss. That's where life took her. I didn't know yet where life would take me. I had no burning cause. I was open to possibility.

I was not afraid of death. Bob and I had talked about it years before, when it was only an abstract thought, not a reality.

"Do you think there is an afterlife?" I had asked him.

"No, I don't," he had said. "Though it is really hard to imagine death. How can you just not exist? I can't feel what that nothing-ness would be like. Scary."

Nothingness didn't frighten me. Dying seemed easy. It was living that was hard. As a child I used to lie awake at night, fearful that something might happen to my parents. Could I exist without them? I no longer felt that terror of being unable to exist without another person. No longer could a death defeat me or overwhelm me. It would change me, but it would not ruin me.

Two of my new friends in the bereavement group were haunted by their husbands' last moments. Julie pictured her husband in a casket. She couldn't let go of that image to remember him at other times, in other places. Marie thought her husband's death was an accident, though he had had cancer for several years and could no longer speak. If only she had been there at the moment of death, maybe she could have saved him. The women asked for help, some words that could take away their pain, but I offered nothing. Later I wondered if their being haunted by their husbands' last moments reflected a fear of their own deaths. Both had said they were afraid to die. "It's okay to go," we had told Bob. I wonder if we were also telling ourselves that it was okay to let him go.

What is a good death? Is it a death like Bob's was, with family members present? Is it a death that ends suffering? Is it a death that does not leave behind agonized mourners? My father and Bob had discussed this years before, when neither of their deaths was imminent. We had just heard a news broadcast: Malcolm Forbes had died suddenly in his sleep. "That's the way to go," my father proclaimed. No pain. No suffering. No illness. Quick and over with in an instant. "Oh, I don't know," Bob had said. "I kind of like the unique way Nelson Rockefeller went."

TWENTY-TWO

$\mathscr{I}$ tried to think about getting back into a real life, a life not filled with illness and fear. Marsha and I went to New York, saw a play, and went to dinner. Bob's friends called and we went to dinner. My friends called and we went to dinner. I cried in every restaurant in New York and New Jersey for the first month. My friends cried with me. Other widows in the bereavement group talked of fleeting thoughts of suicide. I was far too conscientious. The closest I could get was not wearing my seat belt.

I pretended at work that things were okay. And they were, when I was at work. It was harder when I was at home. The emptiness was palpable. There were many things to do, and all of them reminded me of Bob: Probate the will, order the grave marker, send thank-you notes, clean out closets, change the car registrations, transfer bank accounts. It seemed never ending.

Time stretched before me like a great black hole, too vast to fill. I went through the motions, making lists and checking off chores as I did them. I had to learn how to shop for groceries again. I needed at least one week's supply of Healthy Choice dinners and cat food. I hoped Bob wasn't watching. I wasn't using coupons.

Bill called one night. "Will you do the eulogy at my funeral?"

"No," I said. "I won't."

"You won't?"

"Don't you even consider dying before I do. You can speak at *my* funeral."

There were superstitions, rudiments of childhood, that I turned to when I wanted something badly. Driving under a railroad trestle while a train roared overhead. Make a wish. Adjusting the turned-up hem of a skirt. Make a wish. Saying the same phrase at the same time as someone else. Make a wish. But now there was nothing to wish for. It was fruitless to wish that Bob were alive. And nothing else mattered.

Michael and I compared notes about grief on a regular basis. I told him: *I feel like I'm doing nothing but surviving these days. I don't like being at home and I don't feel involved at work. Nothing much appeals to me now. You are one of the few people I never have to pretend with. Thank you for being there all these months, and especially now. Grief is so self-absorbing, and I feel a little embarrassed that I just want to be self-absorbed. I have nothing at all to give to anyone else right now.*

Michael: *Nothing is supposed to appeal to you right now. Self-absorbed is exactly where you are supposed to be. You are appallingly normal. I am happy to help you in whatever way I can. Going through this with you is helping me to face some issues that I need to face before I can move on with my life. So I should be thanking you. Thank you.*

The bereavement group was like an island in the middle of a swamp. Once a week I would wade through the muck and mire to safety. I liked that my fellow bereaved were at different stages in their grief. Something to look forward to or look back on, a process. It helped me to cry for others, too. I felt grateful that I didn't have small children to worry about, that I could pay my bills, that I had a job, that I could usually get a good night's sleep. No one in the bereavement group cooked. Why bother? "I guess this group won't be having any potluck dinners," said John, one of our members.

There were two kinds of widows—I was now taking regular polls—those who went to the movies alone but not out to dinner, and those who could go to a restaurant alone but not to the movies. I was a movies widow. It surprised me that I couldn't go to restaurants alone, since I often did so on business trips. I just couldn't do it in my hometown.

Odd little things cropped up, feelings I wasn't sure were normal. I took them either to the bereavement group or to Michael: *Tell me if you think this is weird. I've been sending thank-you notes to friends who made donations in Bob's memory. Both of our names are on the address stickers. I have used most of the stickers up, and it is really upsetting me. I have this terrible anxiety that when I use them all up, it will mean that Bob is really gone. Of course, I could order more with his name on them, but that doesn't seem to be the right thing to do. So I've decided I will not use them all up. I'll keep some around so that Bob will always be here.*

I realized that this was what grief is and why it is such a difficult task. It requires us to let go and to hold on at the same time.

Michael wrote back: *You just put those stickers aside and save them forever. When I finally started going through Greg's things— and I haven't finished, even now—I found his box of personal checks. I was going to keep them, but then I thought, "This is ridiculous. He's never going to write another check." So I sat there, crying, ripping them up book by book. I don't know why I put myself through all that. I wish now that I had just saved them and decided later what to do.*

I was still getting condolence notes. My favorite was from Ben, a friend of Bob's whom I didn't know very well. It made me laugh out loud. Bob had used two different names. His first name was Raymond, after his father, and his middle name Robert, after an uncle. His family had always called him Bob. Coworkers had called him Ray. On his first job after college, people called him Raymond since that was how he signed things. At age twenty-one, he said, he wasn't assertive enough to correct them. Throughout our marriage it was a game for me to try to predict when he would introduce himself as Bob and when he would call himself Ray. Ben wrote:

Dear Gail,

I had been meaning to write to Ray for a while and just hadn't gotten around to it. I seem to be so busy with trivial things that I don't get around to anything that is important.

About ten times in the past year, a sports question came up that I couldn't answer. Each time it did, I thought about calling Ray. He would have known. I have such fond memories of him. As you undoubtedly know, he was not your average person. From 1965 to 1967, we had desks next to each other at Mutual Benefit. There was a dichotomy between how seriously he took his work and his personal life. He is the only person I know who regularly changed lanes in the Lincoln Tunnel. While I was not acquainted with all his friends, I can say with great certainty that you were quite a change from the females with whom he used to associate. Not to disparage them, I was surprised and delighted to note that he had doubled his average female-companion IQ points when you and he got together.

Sincerely,
Ben

I marveled at the different feelings expressed in the bereavement group. And I was even more delighted to learn that all the widows had been married to saints. I hadn't known there were so many saints in the world, much less in New Jersey. It was not hard for me to relate to all the sadness and pain, but the anger confounded me.

When I was very young I asked my mother about the inequities of life. "How can some people be born into a family of psychologists," I said, "and others be born into a family of garbagemen?" The lowest station I could think of in my middle-class suburban town. Life isn't fair, I believed it even then. Never has been. Never will be. How can you rage at bad luck?

Other widows in the bereavement group felt differently. They were furious at their husbands for dying, just like my mother-in-law. They were furious at God. They were furious at doctors and hospitals. And my friend Joan was furious that anyone older than her husband could still be alive. "How dare he be here. He must be eighty years old. My husband wasn't even seventy."

TWENTY-THREE

$\mathcal{I}$ was invited to Marsha's for Rosh Hashanah in September. She wanted to provide me with family, and I think she secretly wanted me to feel as Jewish as she thought I ought to be. I hadn't seen her family since Bob's illness. They offered condolences. I cried a little. Marsha said, "Since Bob's not here, I put mushrooms in everything." I wondered if anyone thought it insensitive to remind me of Bob's absence. But she knew, being a widow herself, that it is better to talk about the missing person than to ignore the absence. It's always there, like the unyielding pain of a toothache. Not commenting doesn't make it go away. Reminding me of Bob's food quirks made me laugh. He could zero in on the tiniest piece of a mushroom like a hawk. And we once lied to him, insisting that Marsha's spinach lasagna had broccoli, not spinach, in it. He didn't eat it. You can't trust anyone but family, and even with family you can't be too careful when it comes to mushrooms and spinach.

In October I got a call from Bob's brother Ron. We started with the weather, as always.

"It's been raining a lot here," he said, "and our neighbors' yards slope into ours. So we have big puddles out back. I'm going to tell them they should have gutters put on their houses, so this doesn't happen."

I wasn't at all prepared for what came next.

"I just got a copy of Bob's will," Ron said.

"I knew you would be getting a copy soon, since you were mentioned in it."

"It was signed in June. How could that have been? You know he wasn't in his right mind in June."

I should have said that I wasn't sure Bob was ever in his right mind. Instead I said, "You're right. He wasn't functioning very well in June."

"So how could he have written a will then?"

"What makes you think that just because he signed the will in June, he hadn't thought about what he wanted to do with his estate long before that?" I then added, because I thought that it would pacify Ron, "He left a bank account to you and Roger, besides what was listed in the will."

That did seem to pacify Ron. But I was furious. I felt bullied. In the twelve years that Bob and I had been married, I had watched Ron humiliate waiters in restaurants when his order wasn't right. I had watched him talk to service people as though their only purpose in life was to serve him, and I had even watched him address his brother, Roger, as "the boy," as in "I'll call 'the boy' to get the squirrels out of my attic."

One Christmas Eve I spoke up. "I'm sick of the way you treat people, and your using words like Jap, nigger, and fag. I don't want my friends referred to that way. If that's how you feel, then keep it under wraps around me." I had worried that Bob might be angry with me for telling Ron what I thought. But he always supported me. Still, I apologized later, especially for speaking out on Christmas Eve when the whole family was supposed to be happily celebrating. I didn't imagine that Ron had forgiven me. He was not used to having anyone, especially a woman, tell him what to do.

Though he didn't state it explicitly—I only found out later from Janet—he believed that I had influenced Bob to include my children in the will, maybe even wrote it myself and coerced Bob to sign it. How meaningless that would have been. The small amount of money that Bob left to my children was completely unimportant. What was important was that this was Bob's last and most profound gift to me, telling me that he cared about my children and considered them part of his family. For Ron, though, generosity was concrete and material. Sentiment and feeling didn't count.

Now I spoke out again. I wrote to Ron, telling him how I felt about his questioning my integrity and my love for Bob. It was incomprehensible to me that his not trusting anyone but family could be carried to this extreme. And I wasn't willing to let this go, or to try to make peace.

I made matters worse. Ron and Mom held the mortgage on our house. I wanted to pay off what I owed so I would never have to write another check to Ron. What I did next was vindictive, but at the time I felt justified. Bob had paid Ron an extra half percentage point in interest each month, more than we had agreed to in our written contract. I decided to pay only the amount stated in the contract. He wasn't going to get a penny more than what he could prove I legally owed. It was a standoff between our attorneys for a month. Finally, knowing that I couldn't win without going to court, and knowing that Bob would certainly have wanted me to pay what he had agreed to, I gave in and paid what Ron's lawyer demanded. I could have guessed that would be the end of our relationship. I never heard from Ron again.

TWENTY-FOUR

$\mathcal{M}$y sons continued to check on me every week, just as they had during Bob's illness. Chris brought me an armload of mysteries. "You'll have lots more time now, Mom. This will help." Books never failed me. They were better than Prozac. A longer half-life.

In the bereavement group we were encouraged to build shrines for our saints. This was where we could hold on to our loved ones. The rest of the world was where we were expected to let go. The social workers in charge invited us to bring in pictures for our shrines. I loved the idea of seeing what the saints looked like and sharing my own pictures. We would pass them around the group, three-by-fives and eight-by-elevens that showed our spouses on cruises or at weddings or in nightclubs.

Taking this assignment seriously, I brought in a poster-size collage that I had asked Jane to make for Bob's memorial service. The pictures seemed like pieces of a jigsaw puzzle that didn't quite fit together. Time became jumbled: Bob at age two with his dad on the front steps of their house, Bob in high school wearing sunglasses and looking like Mr. Cool. A picture with me and his mom at Montezuma Castle where Roger worked as a park ranger. Bob with the cats at the kitchen table.

There were pictures of Bob with others and pictures of Bob alone. Standing by Harrods in London. At the Jersey shore with his yellow Bermuda shirt, the one with the rows of tiny liquor bottles on it. Wearing his Penn State sweatshirt. There was even a picture of Bob during his first marriage twenty years before, holding his little bichon frisé, Bobby. Bob was the only person I'd ever met who had named his dog after himself.

In one picture, gentle Bob held my mom's hand in the nursing home. I remembered looking at the picture last December, thinking how frail my mother looked and how it might be her last Christmas. I had never imagined it would be Bob's last, too.

And there was a picture of Bob and me with Ron and Jane, just before they moved to Albuquerque. It had been October then, just as it was now.

Autumn had always been my favorite season. That clean crisp air, days neither too hot nor too cold. And the leaves in all hues. I didn't think of them as dying, though they surely were. I thought of them as blazing in glory, triumphant, showing their true colors. I could almost remember, in a Proustian sort of way, the smell of burning leaves from bonfires many years ago, back when we didn't know that burning leaves was harmful. Now I could hardly believe how my life had changed. The foreshortened days brought yearning. I thought back to the year before. Columbus Day weekend. Bob and I had driven to New Hampshire to see the leaves and try to find the camp I had attended as a child. As we sailed along the highway in Connecticut, sunroof open, holding hands, singing along with the radio, I looked out over the spectacular countryside, hills sparkling with a rainbow of greens, yellows, oranges, and reds. I leaned over, kissing Bob on the cheek, and said, "It just doesn't get any better than this, does it?"

We had paid for this comfort and passion with our early years of conflict. What a cruel twist of fate to have the marriage we had worked so hard for vanish in the space of five months.

In the bereavement group, another widow, Marie, told her story. Her husband had been an alcoholic for the first seventeen years of their marriage. There were many nights when she wished that it could be over, that he wouldn't come home. But for the last seventeen years he had gone to AA, become a sponsor for others in recovery, and transformed into a kind and loving husband—more than paying her back for the agony of the early years. This love, which had been strengthened by hard times, seemed deep, and the loss profound. It is the contrasts that make us appreciate what we have. Spring is more glorious after a cold, bleak winter.

I wrote to Michael: *This is the two-month anniversary of Bob's death. Do you ever stop counting months in this way?*

Michael writes: *I think I just recently stopped counting the months. Now I count the seasons, and soon, I guess, I will start counting years. Time really does help, but it's such a slow process. One evening you'll say to yourself, "I didn't think about Bob at all today." Then, if you're like me, that will make you uncomfortable and set off some new stage of grieving.*

TWENTY-FIVE

$\mathcal{I}$ hadn't gone to the bereavement group to make friends, really. Just to find comfort. But I did begin to make friends. In particular, I looked forward to seeing Joan. Joan was one of those Upper West Side liberals who wanted to save humanity but didn't much care for any of its individual members. And she was given to saying outrageous things about who should and who shouldn't have died. But she made us all laugh. Each week she would regale us with her daily problems in living.

"I never learned how to cook in forty-five years of marriage," she told us. "I don't even know how to shop for food. Last night I threw out everything in the refrigerator. It had been there half an hour and I wasn't sure if it might have gone bad. I couldn't take any chances that my children would be orphaned."

The next week she told us how her car had gotten stuck at the top of a hill just as she was starting out to visit her daughter. "What do I know about cars?" she said, as we widows all nodded in understanding. "I don't even know what kind of car I have. All I know is that it's red." The next week it was a problem with the furnace.

"If all else fails," I told her, "you could always do stand-up comedy."

Joan was a restaurant widow. It was the only way she could manage to eat, she said. We sometimes would go to the movies together. Once she looked around the theater and proclaimed, "You know, there really should be a law about people going out in couples. I think they should require all the men to sit on one side and the women on the other, just like in an Orthodox synagogue. I'm going to go speak to the management about this right now. And if anyone complains I will just call them anti-Semitic."

Joan thought that I was a competent widow. I could cook. I could clean. I knew how to write checks to pay my bills. I could drive in New York City. I was her role model until she discovered that I didn't know how to spin lettuce dry in a salad spinner. This was one of her skills. Now we were on more equal footing.

The rest of us were also mastering the skills of living alone. I discovered there were even a few advantages to being by yourself. You could eat ice cream directly out of the carton, you didn't have to shut the bathroom door, and you could turn the light on in the middle of the night if you had a sudden thought you wanted to write down.

Nights could be difficult. Some of us dreamed. Two of the women in the bereavement group never dreamed of their departed husbands. They smelled their husbands' cologne or the smoke from their cigarettes and sensed their presence in other ways. Some of us heard our husbands' voices in our minds, telling us we could get through this, they were proud of us, they were watching. Julie dreamed of her husband Mike. "My Mike," she called him. She often dreamed that he told her he was coming for her. She would wake up feeling pleased and immediately set about cleaning her apartment. Just in case. Did our mothers all tell us the same thing? "Be prepared. Don't wear torn underwear. . . ."

I did dream. Just a little. Ordinary dreams of Bob and me going to a restaurant with friends, raking leaves, driving in the car. A wish, surely, for our everyday life together as it had been a year before. And I would feel Bob's presence when I was awake. I imagined him lying in bed with me with his arms around me, as they had been every night. I stroked his beard. I threw one leg over his. It was as close as I could get. I felt him the way one might feel a phantom limb after the real one had been amputated.

Halloween came and went. "Yours is the best house," the neighborhood kids had stated year after year. Of course it was the best house. Bob bought candy bars the size of legal envelopes. And he puffed with pride at being the best house. Undoubtedly all the dentists and pediatricians in town thought it the best house, too. In memory of Bob, I dispensed huge candy bars and maintained our reputation.

TWENTY-SIX

$\mathscr{I}$ was still counting months. I knew that November would be hard. It was the start of the holiday season, and Bob's birthday was in November. I was preparing myself, carefully avoiding certain aisles in the stationary store. *Happy Birthday to My Dear Husband. Happy Thanksgiving to My Wonderful Wife.*

Several weeks before Thanksgiving was my yearly checkup with the gynecologist. I felt sure I would find a shoulder to cry on. We'd had a relationship for thirty years. And he'd delivered both my children. Every year he teased me, "I thought you remarried. Why don't you use your husband's last name? Doesn't he care that you still use your first husband's name?"

Every year I answered, "No, he doesn't. He's very secure."

But this time he just said, "How are you?" Expecting, no doubt, the usual answer, "Fine."

"I've been having a hard time," I told him. "My husband died in August."

"What did he die of?" he asked in his most professional fashion.

"A glioblastoma," I said. "He was sick for five months."

There was a long, weighty silence. It was hard for me to believe that he couldn't just say, "I'm sorry." Isn't that what we've all learned to say when we can't think of any other words?

Instead he said, "Divorced from your first husband. And your second one dies. I guess you just can't keep a man."

I gasped. The rest of the visit proceeded in silence. I wanted to give him the benefit of the doubt, believing that he wished he hadn't said it. I waited for an apology, some acknowledgment. But there was none. I was horrified that he could joke so cavalierly about my husband's death. Not only that, but he'd tapped into a fear. Maybe I couldn't keep a man. Maybe I couldn't keep a gynecologist, either. I found a new one.

The short, gray November days felt right for grief. Attendance was high at the bereavement group. We looked, we widows, for signs from our husbands from the great beyond. One of our group went to visit a psychic, hoping to communicate with her husband that way. One weekend, I, too, wondered if there were ghosts. Both the smoke alarm and the telephone rang for no apparent reason. There was no smoke, since I didn't cook, and no caller. The telephone wouldn't stop ringing even when I picked up the receiver.

My friend Marsha said, "It's probably Bob trying to reach you."

"Damn," I said. "I knew I should have gotten call-waiting."

I believed that Bob's birthday would be my hardest day so far. I did better with hard days when I planned ahead. I sent Mom flowers with a note, "Thanks for the gift you gave me fifty-five years ago today." I wrote Bob a letter, but I didn't know where to send it. I stood beside his grave and read aloud a poem that my friend Ernie had shared with me years before. It spoke to me of life's evanescence.

STRANGE HOLINESS
by Robert P. Tristam Coffin

There is a strange holiness around
Our common days on common ground.

I have heard it in the birds
Whose voices reach above all words,

Going upward, bars on bars,
Until they sound as high as stars.

I have seen it in the snake,
A flowing jewel in the brake.

It has sparkled in my eyes
In luminous breath of fireflies.

I have come upon its track
Where trilliums curled their petals back.

I have seen it flash in under
The towers of the midnight thunder.

Once, I met it face to face
In a fox pressed by the chase.

He came down the road on feet,
Quiet and fragile, light as heat.

He had a fish still wet and bright
In his slender jaws held tight.

His ears were conscious whetted darts,
His eyes had small flames in their hearts.

The preciousness of life and breath
Glowed through him as he outran death.

Strangeness and secrecy and pride
Ran rippling down his golden hide.

His beauty was not meant for me,
With my dull eyes so close to see.

Unconscious of me, rapt, alone,
He came, and then stopped still as stone.

His eyes went out as in a gust,
His beauty crumbled into dust.

There was but a ruin there,
A hunted creature, stripped and bare.

Then he faded at one stroke,
Like dingy, melting smoke.

But there his fish lay like a key
To the bright lost mystery.

It surprised me that going to the cemetery brought such comfort. I watched as a flock of gray birds landed at a gravesite near Bob's. As I was about to leave, they lifted in a perfect V and soared away. What Bob had taught me about love and generosity would live forever in me and, I hoped, in the people whose lives I touched.

Once I had asked my friend Jane, "Which would you rather be—loved or respected?" She liked that choice better than the one I had given her the week before, "Which would you rather be—fat or bald?" She didn't hesitate. "Loved, of course." I agreed with her now.

I left the cemetery, drove home, and put on the Penn State game. That's what Bob would have done on this Saturday. But I didn't watch the game in quite the same way he would have, moving closer and closer to the television, trying almost to get inside, believing that proximity could influence the score if the game weren't going the right way. This time it did. Penn State won. For Bob.

Thanksgiving followed immediately after Bob's birthday. I went to Michigan to be with my brother and his family. Thanksgiving had always been the holiday that we spent with my family. Christmas was with Bob's. This year would be no different. Except, of course, Bob would not be there.

Sitting around the table before my brother carved the turkey, we took turns stating what it was that we were most thankful for. It was hard for me to see my half-full glass. I felt so empty.

TWENTY-SEVEN

$\mathcal{B}$ack in October, before my final exchange with Ron, I had begun to think about Christmas.

"You know," I told Marsha, "I'd really like to spend Christmas with Bob's family." In fact, I couldn't envision *not* spending Christmas with Bob's family. We had always celebrated Christmas long and hard, with food and gifts starting in late morning and ending late at night. This family could win the prize for the commercialization of Christmas. Every year we would vow to cut down on the number of gifts, and every year we all got everything we had ever wanted and then some. After twelve years, I couldn't imagine Christmas any other way.

"Why don't you tell them you want to spend the holiday with them?" Marsha said. "I think they'd be pleased that you still want to be part of the family."

It was hard to ask for what I wanted. I had never had to with Bob; he always seemed to anticipate my needs. But with Marsha's coaching I convinced myself that they might want it, too, and that it wouldn't be an imposition.

As usual, I sent out my yearly Christmas letter. Two years earlier I had chosen a "restaurant review" theme; the December before Bob died I did "the ABCs of Christmas," starting with *A . . . Acer Computer. My big investment this year. I refuse to let technology get the best of me. But why does all this time-saving technology take so much time?* Through *Z . . . Zero problems. That is what we wish for you.*

This year I had to inform friends and distant family, those I only wrote to at Christmas, about Bob's and my mother's death. To inform them that the wish for zero problems hadn't come true for us. I found it hard to let people know in a way that wouldn't shock or seem maudlin. In fact, I hadn't been able to talk about it yet with everyone at work. You can't just start a conversation with, "My husband died in August."

I arrived in Sedona several days before Christmas, my luggage vacationing in Las Vegas for a day and a half. Immediately I felt the tension of the family rift. Ron had issued a directive demanding that Mom and Roger, out of respect for him, should end their relationship with me. I was pleased that they chose not to do so, but I also knew that they felt guilty. For the first time since they moved to Albuquerque, Ron and Jane had stayed there for Christmas.

Roger had flown to New Jersey to pick up a new puppy, their third Lab, from the breeder. The puppy was replacing Bowie, who'd been with them for twelve years but was now with Bob. Roger and I weren't able to get on the same flight to Phoenix. Mine arrived first, so I waited for him in the airport. He was tense and exhausted when his delayed flight finally arrived.

The combination of the long flight, the new puppy, and, probably, some conflicting feelings about my visit made him irritable. "Next year we're sending you a fruit basket, and sending Mom to Albuquerque with Ron and Jane. Janet and I will stay home alone for Christmas," he said.

The next morning, Mom arrived for breakfast. Her tension was obvious, too. "Hi, Briddie!" she said as she bent down to play with the new puppy. "Oh, hello Gail," she added, almost as an afterthought. I couldn't decide which felt worse, being there without Bob or being persona non grata. Roger and Mom seemed to be struggling, too, all of us trying to decide what our new roles in the family were. Bob's absence left a big, gaping hole, and no one knew what to do about it. Janet and I were the only ones who seemed to understand each other. Later, hoping we could discuss the problems more openly, I mentioned Ron to Roger. He stormed out of the room. "I don't wish to talk about it," he said angrily on his way out.

Later I wrote to Michael: *I'm not sure what kind of a relationship I will have with my in-laws now. Do you have any relationship with Greg's family?*

Michael: *My family totally accepted Greg, but his family never accepted me. They didn't like gay people, or white people. I don't think I ever told you that Greg was black.*

This is what I imagined it felt like to be part of a group that was discriminated against. It seemed that my very presence caused discomfort, and it had little to do with what I did or who I was.

The gift-giving this year lasted an hour. But it eased the tension, at least. Roger had asked months before if he could have one of Bob's shirts. I brought Bob's Penn State sweatshirt for Roger, another of Bob's shirts for Janet, and for Mom the classy Sedona hat that she had given Bob, along with the bolo tie that he had worn at Roger and Janet's wedding.

Roger and Janet gave me a book of Christmas stories entitled *This Year Will Be Different,* by Maeve Binchy. We all cried then. We missed Bowie and Bob, picturing them together somewhere eating Christmas dinner, Bob spooning up rice pudding with raisins and Bowie lapping up her rice pudding without. Mom missed Ron and Jane, too.

After dinner, Roger and Janet took the dogs for a walk while Mom and I settled in for a long talk. We spoke as peers, fellow widows. I waited for her to tell me about the pain of losing a son, but she didn't.

"When my husband died, I stayed in the house for two years," Mom said. "I never went anywhere unless I had to. Finally, people told me I had to start doing things. I went back to work in the family real estate business. And I started going to Parents Without Partners."

"Isn't that where you met Sam?" I asked. I had never met Sam, but Bob had spoken of him often.

"No, I met him somewhere else."

"How come you didn't marry him?"

"He was a nice man, but I just didn't love him."

I wondered then if she and Bob's dad had had the kind of love that Bob and I had had. Bob must have learned to love somewhere.

"I don't imagine that I'll ever get married again, either," I said.

"Well, it is better not to get married for the wrong reasons." Whatever they were.

TWENTY-EIGHT

$\mathcal{W}$e went to church on Christmas Eve. It felt so right to me that I thought I ought to consider going to church more often. I hadn't gone since high school, and I wasn't quite sure how to start again. I thought about the Unitarian Church my parents went to. The church, my mother had said, where "the only time you heard the word God was when the janitor stubbed his toe."

Bob and I had met in a Unitarian Church, which amazed our friends and relatives when we told them. We laughed at the expressions on their faces. In truth, we had sat in a little room up on the third floor of the church annex, having dragged our folding chairs upstairs with us. It was a singles' discussion group.

We were assigned a topic to discuss, something like "an unexpected event that happened in your life." When Bob spoke, I felt a knot in my stomach, anxiety on his behalf. He described how he had felt the day his wife left him. The man sitting next to me leaned over and whispered, "He is very brave to be able to say that." Almost all of us in the group had been divorced, but only Bob talked about it. It scared me that he could be so open with a roomful of strangers about something so painful. When it was my turn to speak, I did just the opposite, joking about how nothing was so unexpected when you got to be as old as I was.

Bob followed me out of the room and down the stairs. "You don't look so old," he said. We compared drivers' licenses. He was three months older than I. He asked if I would go to dinner with him the next evening, but I was busy. From that moment on, he pursued me. Love at first sight, he told me. Not for me. But I agreed to go out with him in spite of the fact that he was wearing orange plaid polyester pants and a pink short-sleeved shirt. It was only later that we found that we had more in common than the years we graduated from college.

I returned to the bereavement group when I got back from Sedona. Julie had sent us all holiday cards, printed from her computer. And for New Year's she sent a picture of a heart with a Band-Aid and a greeting: *May the new year bring peace to your heart.* Elaine, the group social worker, had told us that the more tears we cried, the closer we would be to healing. I thought I should be pretty much healed, given all the boxes of tissues I had used. One evening, at a candlelight memorial service sponsored by hospice, a member of our group dropped her lighted candle. At last we had a use for all the wet Kleenex we carried with us every day.

We talked about the new year. What it would bring for us. Dolores did not want to say goodbye to 1996. It was the last year that her husband would ever be part of. I was glad to see 1996 end. It was hard not to hope that the coming years would be better. But I, too, couldn't let 1996 go so easily. I had a big erasable calendar hanging on the refrigerator, the center of communication, America's version of the European kiosk. The calendar showed all the dates for Bob's many treatments and doctors' appointments. I couldn't just erase all this and start over. It went in the Bob box along with my address labels, condolence cards, and old pictures and notes that Bob and I had given to each other. I bought a 1997 calendar to hang on the refrigerator. A new year, not a recycled one.

Above the calendar was a card from the funeral home with the words of the Serenity Prayer, *God, grant me the serenity to accept the things I cannot change . . . ,* and the dates of Bob's existence, November 23, 1941–August 19, 1996. The hyphen was what it was all about. Birth and death. And points in between.

I had two hobbies now. The first was checking left hands each week in the bereavement group. Who was and who was not wearing a wedding ring. This had been the topic of discussion one week. Even after I had separated from my first husband, I hadn't wanted to be single. I agonized over the proper time to remove my rings. Then, one day, I just did it. I didn't want to think about it anymore. This time I was in no hurry. The decision didn't trouble me. I would, I decided, just let it evolve. I'd take my rings off when it felt right. Maybe soon, maybe never.

My second hobby was checking the obituaries in the *New York Times* every day. The *Times* was the only paper I read that listed cause of death. Curiously, though, it was rarely noted for people over eighty, as if it didn't matter what you died of if you were old. I checked to see how many people had died of cancer, and more specifically if any had died of a brain tumor. There weren't many, but I felt a special affinity for those that I found. I knew something of that journey, and I imagined what it had been like for them.

TWENTY-NINE

$\mathcal{I}$t had been a whole year since the first brain tumor symptoms, our trip to Arizona, and my mother's death. Before we had known how sick Bob was, we had taken our last trip together. For Valentine's Day. It had been a wonderful jaunt, a diversion in the middle of the week, to the Mirror Lake Inn at Lake Placid. It was cold and snowy when we left and even colder and snowier when we got there. We bundled up for a romantic walk, Bob revisiting the haunts from his ski trips many years before. After dining early in the handsomely appointed restaurant, the fireplace ablaze across the room and our table overlooking the verandah to the snow-covered lake, we retired to our room and stretched out on the bed to open the valentine gifts we had brought. "This is so much fun," we agreed. "Let's make this a tradition. Let's go away every year for Valentine's Day."

So here it was, Valentine's Day again. But where was my valentine? This had become the saddest day of my year. The only day that Bob and I had celebrated by ourselves and for each other. We would go to our favorite restaurant, Union Square Cafe, or find a new, more romantic one. I couldn't bear to be reminded, to see the flower deliveries and the heart-shaped balloons. The rest of the world could celebrate—it wasn't my holiday anymore. I took the day off from work and went to the cemetery with a rose.

John, from the bereavement group, told us a touching story. A year ago he had bought very special roses, pale yellow with just a tinge of red edging on each petal, for his partner, Jerry. Jerry loved them so much that he dried them and kept them. When Jerry died in July, John had looked for more. Serendipitously, the florist had gotten another delivery by mistake. So John bought them all for Jerry's funeral, knowing that's just what Jerry would have wanted. This year, John had no one to give roses to. He thought about all the widows in the bereavement group and decided to make each of us a perfect red origami rose. It was a rose that would last forever. No one needed roses more than the members of our group.

Michael wrote me a note: *Will you be my valentine?*

And I wrote back: *But of course. Will you be mine? Thank God for friends.*

This is what Valentine's Day would be for me now. I would hang out with others who hated the holiday because they didn't have a partner. And I would do what Jews did on Christmas. Eat Chinese food and go to the movies.

Michael struggled, too, with being single and alone: *Even more than on Valentine's Day, I miss Greg on Sunday afternoons when football games are on TV, or at night when I am in my vast, empty waterbed. It has only been recently that I say "I" instead of "we." I sadly feel that there is no hope for any future relationship.*

I replied: *Why is it that you feel no hope for another relationship? I want you to have another fulfilling relationship as much as my friend Marsha wants me to have one. But why is it that we think other people need this? I don't even know what I need sometimes, much less what anyone else needs.*

Marsha reminded me of what it was like to be part of a couple. I missed the mundane things that couples did together: discussing the day's events over dinner, checking with each other to schedule social engagements, even arguing over who's going to do which chores. When Marsha went shopping for furniture with her husband, I sent a note to her and Michael: *Bob and I did okay when we went furniture shopping together, but the furniture we brought into the marriage certainly reflected our different tastes.*

Bob had an awful leopard-skin couch that he just loved. I finally was able to convince him to let me cover it in a conservative brown and relegate it to the basement recreation room.

Michael responded: *Leopard-skin couches. Hmmm. There is something awfully familiar about that. Tell me about Bob again?*

I wrote: *Well, if you're implying. . . . Well, maybe he was and I never knew it. I really doubt it, though. He sure did like women. I don't think he could possibly have faked that kind of admiration, not to mention performance.*

Michael: *Hey, if the performance was there, who cares if he was or wasn't? I'm just kidding—he sounds like a wonderful, sensitive man. I wish I had known him. He's just the sort of man I'd expect you to be with.*

Marsha had the final word: *Now you have got to be kidding. If Bob hadn't been so in love with you, Gail, I think he would have been in love with every other woman. Bob just plain loved females, and that's all there is to that.*

My birthday was the week after Valentine's Day. I told myself that if I could just get through the month, I would feel better. This is what I told myself every month, but February was the toughest.

Joan looked around the room one night in the bereavement group. "You know," she said, "I really think it would make more sense if people died at the same time that their loved ones died. Then we wouldn't have to have groups like this." I thought about this for a minute. It occurred to me how interconnected we all were. Six degrees of separation. I supposed the whole human race would have to die at once. Maybe a case could be made.

But I was glad that my kids were still around and that we didn't all have to die at the same time. They celebrated my birthday that year in the same way that Bob might have. Tim sent flowers to my office; Chris took me out for dinner and gave me a plant and a card with one of the first sentimental notes he had ever written to me:

Dear Mom,

I hope that your birthday is a very special day. You have always given me so much all of my life, and I hope to start doing the same for you. May all of your days, months, and years be special—like you are.

Love always,
Chris

Birthdays in Bob's family were celebrated in the same lavish way that Christmases were. I wondered how many waiters and waitresses were driven to other jobs after one of our birthday parties. The celebrant would choose a restaurant for the birthday dinner. When we got there, Mom would read the menu and intone in her deep voice, "Nothing here I can eat." On my birthday, I didn't want to be responsible for her inability to find something that appealed to her, so I usually asked Bob to choose the restaurant, or I chose one of the two or three restaurants Mom liked, all of which I hated. The person who had had the previous birthday celebration would open up the "birthday bag," put up the Happy Birthday banner—which usually necessitated getting tape or thumbtacks from the restaurant staff—then place a ceramic slice of cake on the table and pin a "Gimme presents" button on the birthday boy or girl. By this time I usually felt like a birthday girl, not a middle-aged woman. Although I hated the public attention, I did like feeling special on my birthday. It was almost worth the embarrassing ritual.

Since I could no longer celebrate my birthday with Bob or his family, I know he would have been pleased that my children made me feel special. I was pleased, too.

My friends tried to distract me from thoughts of Bob's absence. Michael wrote: *Happy Birthday. On this day, back in 1942, a little miracle occurred and Gail was brought forth into the world, wrapped in swaddling clothes and offered gifts of frankin-cense and . . . oops, wrong story.*

Marsha added: *Pretty funny, Michael. But why was it the wrong story? It was probably the gifts, right?*

This time I had the last word: *Well, it's hard to get frankincense over the counter. But the swaddling clothes are about right. Or is it waddling clothes?*

At the end of February, Joan and I went to see the new Woody Allen movie, *Everyone Says I Love You.* Joan couldn't go to any movie that wasn't billed as a comedy, she said. Still, we were the only two people in the theater who came out crying. The scenes of Venice reminded her of a trip she took with her husband, Alex, and her children. She recalled that the children had played in the Piazza. For me, scenes of the Seine brought back memories of a Paris trip that Bob and I took for our tenth anniversary. Joan and I cried because not everyone was saying "I love you." Alex and Bob weren't.

THIRTY

J went to the bereavement group faithfully every week from September until March. Elaine, the social worker, began each meeting in the same way. "Let's go around the room and say our names and who died for us."

"No one died for us," I wanted to tell her. "They died in spite of us." Maybe there was something religious I was missing, like Jesus dying for our sins.

I was having different dreams now. Dreams of illness. It was my deepest fear, that I would get sick and be alone with no one to take care of me in even small and concrete ways, like driving me to the hospital. I dreamed that I had a brain tumor. The doctor started making plans for surgery and I said, "No. Just let it be. I'm going to go home. There's no one to take care of me. I know what this is like. It will be easier if I just let it take its course as quickly as possible."

Joan asked me one day, "Do you hold on to the banister when you go down the stairs?"

"Yes," I said. "I do."

"I am so careful now," she said. "So afraid of falling. It's like being pregnant. What if we get hurt or get sick? Who will take care of us?"

I worried also that I would die and no one would find me. That I might vanish into thin air. Marsha no longer worked in the same office with me, but she said she'd send me an e-mail every morning when she got to work. And if I didn't answer she'd send the police to my house.

"But what if I die on a weekend?" I asked.

"Just try to hold on until Monday," she advised.

It was at home, isolated and alone, that I felt most invisible. Being with others felt safer. Even vacations, as fraught with anxiety as they could sometimes be, would mean there'd be other people around. If I died in a plane crash, at least someone would know.

My brother had assured me that there would be vacations again. When he invited me to join him, Jackie, and our cousins on a cruise, it had seemed like a good idea. But now I wasn't so sure. I was discovering something new about traveling as a single person: they charge you almost double. I had learned from Bob never to pay extra if you didn't have to, so I decided to let the cruise line find me a roommate. They put me with a lovely seventy-year-old widow from Louisville, who turned out to be the best part of the trip. We bonded instantly, discussing widowhood, travel with our families, and how we wanted their companionship but didn't want to burden them.

It was strange not to be part of a couple, to wonder always if the people you were with saw you as someone they had to take care of in some way because you didn't have a spouse taking care of you. I had always thought of myself as a separate person with my own identity. Why, I wondered, did I not think so now?

It hadn't felt like this before the cruise. I had spent the previous weekend in Florida with my friends Kathy and Meredith. Ladies' Day, we used to call it when we lived closer to each other and could get together every few months. Now it was Ladies' Weekend, since we lived so far apart. The pleasure that I found in the company of women was solid. Women, my friends, could be counted on to understand. There was nothing that we couldn't discuss. The three of us, so different. Yet, soul sisters. Meredith, the intellectual college professor, and Kathy, all impulse and feeling. With me in the middle somewhere.

We talked of the Ladies' Day book we would write together someday. We ate seafood. We got up at five in the morning to watch the sunrise, all bundled up in blankets. Meredith, shedding her intellectual persona for a sensuous self, offered to give us massages. Kathy, in her own role reversal, hung back, revealing a more cautious part of her personality. We laughed, we drank wine, we talked, far into the breezy Florida night, about husbands past and present, and vowed we would do this every year.

I couldn't recreate that sense of companionship on the cruise. At the dinner table I befriended a lonely elderly widower, thinking it an extension of the bereavement group. He mistook my interest as an overture, it seemed. After that I spent my energy avoiding him during the day. I wanted someone to cry with, not to date. I would stand by the railing, watching the red sun sink below the horizon, sure that the waves were two feet higher with the salt water that I was adding.

When I got home from the cruise I headed for the cemetery, one of three places that I could find refuge. The cemetery, where I could talk to Bob, and therapy or the bereavement group, where I could talk about Bob.

"Will we ever heal?" Julie asked one Tuesday night at the bereavement group.

"Yes," I said, "I think we will heal, but there will be a scar. Scar tissue is strong and it looks different. We'll be different. Maybe stronger. But yes, I believe we will heal."

I was becoming adept at filling up the time and space. I just couldn't fill up the hole in my heart. The emptiness was there. No matter how much I ate. No matter how much activity I planned. We, in the bereavement group, talked about the ways we were learning to take care of ourselves, the skills we had mastered. "We've done it. We've become the people you would have wanted us to become. So you can come back now. We've passed the test." We wanted our husbands to be proud of us. We also wanted them to be here.

Michael wrote about loneliness: *I've learned over the past few years that I really have no desire for another relationship. I feel as though my last one was so intense that why even bother with another. Besides, a relationship is work, especially when it's new. I hate those years of breaking someone in. And it takes me a long time to love somebody.*

I thought it more likely that it took him a long time to find the right person to love. I wrote: *Don't you ever feel so alone that it's worth breaking in someone new? I remember how, after I got divorced, I said all the things that you are saying now. But then, after about two years of being alone, I was walking in the park one day and saw a couple kissing. To imagine never again having someone to kiss like that left me with a heart-stabbing loneliness. I cried about it for days. A friend reminded me that waiting for someone to come along would never fill that emptiness. I needed to make myself more available. I did. Then I met Bob. Before I knew what hit me, I had fallen so much in love that he could have been an ax murderer and I still would have been hooked. Thank God he wasn't. I can't imagine ever being in love like that again, but I am not going to say never.*

In April, John offered to teach the widows how to make origami roses. We were all thumbs, like preschoolers learning to cut and paste. "How do you get that leaf folded right? I have a new respect for the Japanese," Joan said. Watching us laugh and play, no one would have recognized us as a bereavement group. And, contrary to John's earlier pronouncement, we did have a potluck dinner. Some of us were cooking again.

Though I was starting to cook for friends, cooking for myself felt slightly self-indulgent. I rated self-indulgences on a scale of 1 to 10. Cooking for myself was a 2. I still ate junk food or Healthy

Choice dinners, depending on my mood, and brought home dog-
gie bags from restaurants. Not having to stop what I was doing to
meet someone else's schedule was a 5 on my scale. Choosing
movies without having to consider someone else's taste rated a 6.

Bob and I had preferred movies on the big screen. We had
trouble making time to watch rentals. But now I liked watching
movies at home. I rented the movie *Shadowlands,* not knowing
what it was about and how deeply it would affect me. I cried so
hard that the front of my shirt was soaked. For once, I was grateful not to be watching it in a theater.

Though crying at movies was not new for me, I was surprised
the one and only time I saw Bob cry there. We'd watched *Field of
Dreams.* He hadn't forgotten his long-lost, sports-loving father.

Now, watching *Shadowlands,* I didn't know from what place
the deep, soul-wracking sobs were coming, just that I couldn't
stop them. The profound love between two very different people,
their unanswerable questions about life and death and the spirit,
and their ability to talk openly about losing each other connected
me to these characters in a way that I will never forget. One of the
characters in *Shadowlands* said, "We read so that we will not be
alone." And we watch movies.

THIRTY-ONE

$\mathscr{I}$t was the end of April, and two more people from the brain tumor support group had said goodbye to family members. A little girl, eight-year-old Cheska, had died. Her Sisyphean father had practically pushed stones up hills to keep her alive. He had guided her treatment with her doctors, learning nearly enough to earn a medical degree. I marveled at his knowledge, his courage, his tenacity. He knew that she would die, but she lived far longer than any of us had expected.

A week or two later, Joe died. Joe was Bob's age, and his glioblastoma had been diagnosed two months before Bob's. I had corresponded regularly with Joe's wife. Knowing they were nearing the end, she called to ask what the dying process would look like. "How sad I am for you that there is nothing more to do," I said. "Please keep in touch with me and let me know how you are." Hard as the caretaking was, letting go was even harder.

I was following one more person in the brain tumor group—Dave Bailey, a brain tumor patient. His youth and maybe his faith had helped him survive two surgeries and experimental chemotherapy. I was amazed at the energy he had. Nothing slowed him down. When Dave was first diagnosed with a glioblastoma, he had turned to songwriting, an old hobby, and formed a duo called Not By Chance with his best friend. He had posted the words to many of their upbeat and emotionally honest songs for the brain tumor group. His fame was spreading. He would soon be on network television, *48 Hours,* and I had already ordered his CD called *Second Chance.*

But now it was time for me to let go of the brain tumor support group. Others needed it more. And I needed to concentrate now on living, not dying.

Illness seems to strike so suddenly. It's hard to remember that when it first comes to our attention, it has been brewing for some time and is not really sudden at all. Like a tulip bulb that will eventually send up green shoots, the potential is there all the while. We just don't know when it will show itself.

Illness and death remind me to live in the moment. That's all I may have. But how quickly I forget this when I live my everyday life. Sometimes it seems that we spend our existence trying to stave off death. My friend Jane once told me I should buy organic produce. "We shouldn't consume any more pesticides than we already have," she said.

"Why?" I asked. "We have to die of something, sometime. Not that I don't want to be healthy. I just don't want to have to worry about dying all the time."

While paying my bills, I noted that all the checks I had written to charities during the year went to groups that enhanced the quality of life for the living: Partnership for the Homeless, CARE, United Way, Gay Men's Health Crisis. Not to those that were working to cure a disease, like the American Heart Association or American Cancer Society. I believed that people could live happier lives. I didn't believe we could stop them from dying.

"What is the meaning of life?" my mother-in-law had asked when her sister died several years ago. "You're born and then you die. For what?" How many others have asked that same question? The meaning of life, I thought, was families and friends sitting around the kitchen table discussing the meaning of life. Like some Zen koan.

At the beginning of May, I went to Houston. I had been there many times on business. Now I had personal relationships there as well. Michael lived in Houston. And whenever I was in Houston I thought of Bob, though he only went with me once.

I remembered how I used to call him at 10:00 P.M. my time, 11:00 his. "Hi, baby," he'd answer, knowing it would be me. I felt like I did when we were first dating and didn't want to say good-bye at the end of the evening. Back then he would call me as soon as he got home, and we'd stay on the phone half the night. As though we were nineteen years old, not forty-two. Hating to say goodbye.

Bob was part of my Houston ritual. I was supposed to call him. He was supposed to meet me at the airport when I got home.

Michael and I drank margaritas and talked about Greg and Bob and moving on.

"Why don't you move down here?" Michael suggested.

"It's a thought," I replied, not entirely dismissing the idea. "I like it here, except for the heat in the summer."

"We could do things together. I really wish you'd come down and keep me company."

"Maybe I will someday." I could move now if I chose to. I was on my own.

Some of the members of the bereavement group were dating now. Some hadn't dated in thirty or forty years. The very word frightened most of us. We decided to call it "meeting new people" rather than dating. A little less threatening. It seemed like blind luck that I had met Bob. To meet someone else would be a mira-cle. I would have as much chance of success, I thought, as I would at winning the lottery. Still, as Ron used to tell the family, you have to be in it to win it. Nonetheless, it wasn't something I was eager to do. Ever.

I watched some of my friends grieve and date at the same time. For me it would be as difficult as simultaneously patting my head and rubbing my stomach, an old childhood challenge. Two sepa-rate motions. How did they do it? And who, I wondered, would dare to date a widow and compete with a saint? It would be much easier to date someone who was divorced and hated her husband

and didn't have pictures of him lined up on every available book-shelf and tabletop.

I wondered if there were husbands who had died who hadn't been canonized. I thought of a story a friend told me long ago. She had been at a party with a couple she knew only slightly. The husband continually berated his wife, Joanne, very publicly. Finally my friend whispered to Joanne, "Don't worry. Someday he'll be dead."

One of the grief books I collected had stated starkly, "Every marriage ends in either death or divorce." It was true, though it had never occurred to me in quite that way before. Loss is inevitable. Someone will always be left behind.

THIRTY-TWO

$\mathcal{B}$y May, I felt that I was beginning to master my bereavement. In fact, I was a little cocky about how well I was doing nine months after Bob's death. I compared myself to the other widows. I was definitely crying less. That seemed to be a first for me, to be in a group where I was the one who cried least. Tears were something I did well, having practiced from early childhood. Almost anything could make me weep: the "Star Spangled Banner," a beautiful sunset, store grand openings, dog shows. And I had never even owned a dog. It wasn't a year yet, and I was beginning to feel better. I had beat the spread, as Bob would have said.

Hubris. It can get you every time.

One day, one of life's little banana peels threw itself in my path. If I didn't know better I'd say that Bob had planted it there.

I come from a family that likes to hand things down from generation to generation. Money, china, values, and even my mother's aphorisms, like, "It's an ill wind that blows nobody good." Or my father's, *"De gustibus non disputandum est."*

My mother had left me a diamond bracelet. I wanted to have it made into a necklace for each grandchild: for Amy and Sara, and for Tim and Chris to give to their wives. Bob had cautioned me, "You might be a bag lady someday. I think you should keep it."

I stood in the jewelry store waiting to speak with the jewelry designer. Suddenly I began to feel lightheaded. I leaned on the counter, took a deep breath, and thought that if the wait were going to be long perhaps I should sit in the car. Then I heard a voice far away saying, "Don't move her. Her head is bleeding."

I looked up, and there, standing above me, were a policeman, all the store employees, and many of the customers. I closed my eyes again, thinking that maybe I could avoid the indignity of it all if I just lay there with my eyes closed. Maybe fainting was what dying was like. You closed your eyes and heard voices in the distance. That didn't seem so bad.

The crowd parted as two emergency technicians, girls who couldn't have been more than fifteen years old, arrived. I thought I owed them an explanation, since I was taking up space on their floor. "I gave blood this morning. I probably should have eaten something before I left the Blood Center."

"Who can we call to come get you?" the fifteen-year-old girls asked.

That started it. The ache that hadn't quite gone away. The vulnerability, the loneliness, and the raw fear. Of abandonment, of separation, of dying alone. Who will help me? Anyone? The fear with the bitter, sour taste, like bile.

"No one. You can't call anyone. My husband is dead," I wailed, needing to tell everyone, "and I live alone." A partner is someone who will come get you if you've been in an accident, someone who will drive you to the hospital if you need to go, someone who will be there to pick up the pieces and console you. There was nothing I could think of that would replace this. My friends weren't around on this holiday weekend. My relatives lived too far away. And, hating to ask for help, I wouldn't have called them anyway. I was beginning to see what a handicap it was to be unable to ask for help when you needed it. I never had to ask Bob for help. He had always been there when I needed him. Now I would have to be, as Tennessee Williams said, forever dependent on the kindness of strangers. If you are going to depend on the kindness of strangers, I reasoned, it is at least good to be able to attract their attention. My ambulance ride home stirred up the neighborhood and brought offers of help.

Still, except for the feelings that surfaced with this accident, I was developing a new life and returning to parts of the old. I not only was cooking again, but I went to two cooking demonstrations with friends, combining my old life with the new. I didn't think I would ever again make rice pudding or strawberry rhubarb pie, though, two of Bob's favorites.

And I began to see therapy patients again in my one-night-a-week practice. During Bob's illness and for a long time afterward, I didn't think I could help anyone. Now I felt strong enough. "I always forget you're a therapist," Joan said. "You seem so sane."

It was Memorial Day weekend, and I was reminded of another death. Two years before, Bob and I had driven to Cape May. A college classmate of mine had died of cancer. She had not been ill long and we were shocked. It didn't seem right that people our age were dying. How could we have known that cancer and death would touch us next?

Carrol and I had kept in touch after college, laughing at our reason for bonding: we had been the only two philosophy majors in our college class. Much to my surprise, after several elegant dinners in Carrol's New York apartment, Bob and Carrol became friends. Bob had found most of my college classmates a little stuffy with their fancy suburban lives and their Wall Street husbands. Our first Christmas together he had asked, "Who are all these people who sent cards?"

"You can figure it out," I said. "The ones who wrote about their horses and where their children are going to prep school are my college friends."

Carrol talked me into going to my twentieth college reunion. I wasn't fond of reunions. They were becoming too expensive. Twice, after comparing myself to my classmates, I'd decided to go back for another degree. But Bob wanted to go to this reunion. I'd let him foot the bill for the next tuition.

We were the talk of the class. At the time, we were living together and not yet married. It was okay to do this, in the Wheaton Class of 1963, it just wasn't okay to talk about it. But the rebel in both of us liked advertising it. And Carrol, who had spent lots of time getting into trouble in college, egged us on. She and Bob had bonded, and together they thumbed their noses—or raised their middle fingers—to propriety. Carrol, of course, did it with perfectly manicured hands.

Soon after Memorial Day weekend, I would be reminded of the other death that I will never quite be able to put behind me. Twenty-four years ago, on June 25, my son Jamie died. He had been healthy at birth. But three weeks later he died of a staph infection. The umbilical cord stump had become infected, spreading systemically. I agonized that I hadn't detected the infection. Never mind that the doctor hadn't, either.

Three weeks isn't a long time in which to create memories. All I have left are some pictures, a baby blanket, his baby book, and a dedication in a book called *Beginnings* that my friend Ellen had written about her own experiences with problem pregnancies and the death of her premature baby.

Jamie would have been a year older than Chris, though as Tim once pointed out at age seven or eight when looking through an old picture album, "If Jamie hadn't died, you wouldn't be here, Chris."

I intervened. "We are all here just by chance, you know. It is really fate, destiny, a happy accident that any of us are here or that we are who we are."

I thought about the twists and turns life takes after a tragedy that we think we can't bear. Though I would never know what kind of a son Jamie might have been, I did know that I could not have loved him more than I loved Chris.

In the bereavement group, I was touched by the things that people did to remember their loved ones. One woman put together a volume of her mother's poems and distributed it to family members. Another man, who didn't talk much in the group, took over some of the things his wife used to do for their grandchildren. His daughter cried when she saw that he had left money in an envelope for the children to go to an amusement park, exactly as her mother used to do.

Julie told us that it had been a year since her husband, Mike, died. She commemorated the date by bringing home flowers and balloons that said *I Love You*. As she entered her apartment with her hands full, the balloons slipped away from her and sailed up to the sky. Three days later, while driving down the Garden State Parkway a few miles from her home, she glanced out her car window. There, floating above her car, were the balloons. She knew that Mike was up there watching over her.

I went home after the group one night and looked around the bedroom. On a bookshelf sat a pair of little red baby shoes. I thought about what Bob was like when he used to wear them, the shoes that his mom had kept for more than fifty years. His recollection of himself as a small child was so different from his mother's. He remembered that he had bright red hair. She said he was a strawberry blonde. He remembered that he was a little hellion who his parents couldn't control. She remembered that he refused to take his coat off when he went to visit relatives. His memories were always a little more intense, a little more pained. That is often the way, I think, of our own memories of ourselves. I found his old baby book with a lock of his hair. It was strawberry blonde.

THIRTY-THREE

*I*n June, my sister-in-law Janet came to visit. It was the first time that I had had an overnight visitor since Bob died. Coming into the house brought back memories for her. We talked a lot about Bob and what it had been like the year before.

"I wish that Roger and I had spent more time with you and Bob without the rest of the family," Janet said. "I think that the four of us would have known each other in a different way."

"I wish that, too," I responded. "I used to ask Bob if he felt left out when you and Roger went out to dinner with Mom, Ron, and Jane, back when you all lived in New Jersey. I wondered if he was sorry you lived within a few blocks of each other while we lived a few counties away."

"Was he?"

"No, actually, he was glad. He was certainly the one who had separated the most from the family. And I don't think I could have lived around the corner from them as you did."

We went to several craft fairs, ate at our favorite restaurants, and planted a hedge of rosebushes. Bob used to dig the holes when we gardened. This time, Janet, the family's master gardener, volunteered to do it. I realized how much I appreciated having someone to do things with for more than a few hours at a time. I had forgotten.

"You're doing so well," Janet said. "What should I tell Mom?"

"I don't know what to tell her. Do you think she would be glad that I'm trying to find a life without Bob? She told me that it took her two years after Bob's dad died before she could go out of the house and do things. Do you think that it's all right if I do it in less than two years? You know Mom."

"Yes, I know her," Janet agreed. "Maybe I won't tell her anything."

I was invited to a party to say goodbye to neighbors who were moving. I made myself go, as I knew it was important to be able to go alone. I sat at a table with some of the neighbors I knew best and tried to make conversation, but I felt awkward, as if I didn't quite belong. Of the twenty-one families on our street, there were only three of us who now lived without a spouse. The other two weren't there. Bob had always had a better time at parties than I did. Although I liked people as much as he did, I was a more solitary person. I would learn, I told myself, to be comfortable in social situations when I had no one to lean on. I didn't have to like it. I just had to do it.

In July, I finally closed Bob's estate. I could at last send Ron his money. I sent it with a note: *Too bad this had to create such hard feelings.* He did not answer. With the checks that I sent Tim and Chris, I enclosed a letter and an extra check of my own—the last joint gift from Bob and me. Tim answered with his own letter:

Dear Mom,

Somehow I'm not quite sure what to say. "Thank you" seems rather inadequate in the face of this generosity, but I suppose it's a start. I'm deeply touched—and to be honest a little uncomfortable. I feel like I'm getting a reward for something I never really was, in a way, and that's disquieting. The actual settlement from the estate (which surprised me in and of itself) was more than generous—to then have you add to it on Bob's behalf is very nearly indescribable. You may rest assured that it will certainly make my and Lisa's life easier. It already has, and it has a way to go yet.

As for appreciating Bob's intangible gifts, I do appreciate many of them, though not all, and I do think that they helped make you an even better mother. Despite all the differences I had with him (and we both know there were quite a few) the one thing that remained absolutely unquestioned was his devotion to you. I was and am very thankful for that.

While I was still living at home, the differences between Bob and me overshadowed everything else. I think I might have recognized his good qualities if we had had more time—unfortunately, we didn't, and I regret that very much.

I wish there were something I could do to make the events of the last two years turn out differently. But we both know there's not. Know, though, that I value your words and your opinions (while reserving the right to stridently disagree with them) and that any-thing I can do to help you in your new life, I will.

Much love,
Tim

I thought back to those years of turmoil in our family and how I had longed for the words that I was hearing now from Tim. There was nothing that I had wanted more than my children's accept-ance of Bob. Bob had wanted that, too. He just hadn't known how to go about getting it. And I hadn't known how to help him. I believed that now, with my children's growing maturity, we would have been able to understand each other.

That July, Chris and Tim each laid claim to five of their fifteen minutes of fame. Tim appeared on a new game show, *Win Ben Stein's Money,* on Comedy Central, and Chris played pool in the background between music videos on VH1. I watched the "History of Music A to Z" on the Fourth of July weekend. Chris appeared in the M's, club-sandwiched between George Michael, Bette Midler, and Mike and the Mechanics. Bob would have loved bragging about both Tim and Chris. I listened closely to the Mike and the Mechanics song, "Living Years."

> Say it loud, say it clear
> You can listen as well as you hear
> It's too late when we die
> To admit we don't see eye to eye

I wondered if Chris had listened to it, too, and if he thought, as I did, that this song said things about his relationship with Bob. No, they did not see eye to eye. Did he wish, like Tim, that he could have told him all he had to say "in the living years"?

THIRTY-FOUR

It was a cool summer. The nights in August felt like early fall. Hard to believe that Bob had been gone almost a year. When I went to the office where I worked in my therapy practice, the psychiatrist talked with me for a few minutes.

"How are you doing now?" he asked.

"Fine," I said.

"Are you really fine? Are you happy?"

"Happy? No, I don't know if I can say that I am happy, though certainly I have moments that are happy. But I wouldn't say that I am unhappy, either."

The next day I talked to Julie on the phone. I told her that I would be leaving the bereavement group soon.

"Everyone is graduating but me," she said.

"You'll graduate, too," I told her. "We all have different graduating classes. Some of us get a GED and some of us skip a semester."

I added pictures of Marsha and Michael to my gallery of photographs. Family is circumscribed. Friends are infinite.

And in the first week of August, I went to Houston again on business. I stayed for the weekend. Michael and I shared a bottle of wine and talked.

"What will we do about this loneliness?" I asked.

"I wish I had met Bob and you had met Greg. Do you think we would have been friends if this hadn't happened to us?"

"Maybe. But it wouldn't have been the same. And it will be different again if we should find other people to love someday."

We drove down to Galveston on Saturday. Being in a car with a man, talking about our lives, our hopes and dreams—it felt so familiar. Like being married. Just for a moment. At night we listened to the Moody Blues. We had the same favorite song, "Isn't Life Strange?" Cry, cry, cry, the song said. We did that, too. Michael polished off the wine. He invited me to stay overnight and share his waterbed. I didn't stay. I didn't think he really wanted me to. Maybe I should have. We both wanted to feel close to someone in that old familiar way.

I knew that it was time for Michael to get involved in a new relationship. He said he was ready. Once he had complained to me, "Mr. Right isn't exactly coming around knocking on my door." I told him, "When he does, you have to be willing to get up and answer it." When it happened, I would miss him. We would always be friends, but, of course, it would be different. We wouldn't be together in our aloneness anymore.

The phone rang on August 15. It was Chris. He asked how I was doing.

"I'm not sure of the exact date of Bob's death," he said. "You sound fine when I talk to you. Are you?"

"Yes, I am. I have moments of sadness. I've been thinking about Bob a lot lately, but I really am okay."

It felt good to have people ask how I was. So often people expect you to have worked through your grief in a few months.

On August 16, flowers came from Mom. "To remember our Bob," the card said. When I called to thank her, we talked of how we missed him, how the year had gone by. How hard it was, still, to believe that he was not here and not coming back. He had been one of the most alive people I had ever met. No one ever failed to notice him.

I thought of Bob again as I watched one of the neighborhood kids walk down the street dressed in green plaid shorts and a red plaid shirt. "But they're both blue," Bob would say when I pointed out his turquoise T-shirt and royal-blue shorts.

New neighbors had moved in next door. Bob would have delighted in two new kids to play with. Michael, age six, followed me into the house.

"Is this your kitchen?" he asked.

Then another question, "Do you have a husband?"

"No," I said. "I used to have a husband, but he died last year. Almost a year ago."

"What did he die of?"

"A brain tumor. Do you know what that is?"

"No. What is it?"

"It's a kind of cancer. A lot of people die of an illness called cancer."

I was astounded at how easily I could talk about this. There is no pretending with children. So matter of fact.

THIRTY-FIVE

*A*ugust 19. Bob had been gone one year. I put on a pair of his old shorts and one of his old T-shirts. I guessed it was one Ron had given him. It was purple and said *New Mexico* across the front. I couldn't quite get myself to wear the yellow Bermuda shirt with the liquor bottles, though I had saved it, of course. It just wasn't me.

I drove to the cemetery. A beautiful sunny day. I sat on the ground, hugging my knees, looking at Bob's grave marker and the pink geraniums that I had planted in May, pleased that they were still blooming and hadn't been mowed over. I sat for a long time thinking about Bob, wondering if he would be happy about his proximity to Giants Stadium. It wasn't a pretty cemetery. There weren't enough trees, for one thing.

Every year, when Bob's family was still in New Jersey, Bob, Mom, and his brothers made a pilgrimage during the first week in December to put grave blankets on the family graves. And every year, Bob, who had a keen sense of direction and was punctual to the half second, got lost and was late. I wondered, as I sat there now, what it was about going to the cemetery that had been so painful for him. I looked at the half of the grave marker that was left empty. It would be engraved with my name someday. I wondered how Tim and Chris would feel about that.

I went home and put a videotape in the VCR. There was Bob, clowning around, large as life. Just an ordinary person, not famous in any way, but very special to me, to his family, to his friends. I wished Roger and Janet had made more tapes of us together. It was good to hear his voice again.

That night I went to the bereavement group to say goodbye. I brought along a note that Michael had written to me the year before, a few weeks after Bob's death: *Will you miss Bob terribly forever? Yes and no, I think. Yes, you will always miss him because you loved him so much. Nobody can ever take that away from you. No, because time is a mighty healer. I think I know you well enough to say that you will be lonely the rest of your life. Powerful love doesn't come along very often, as you already know. You may find somebody else, and I hope you do, but there is always going to be that void—missing and loving Bob. Sad, but true, I believe. Sorry to tell you this, but in some ways, honey, you're never going to get over this. It will just soften until it is a "jagged little pill."*

Michael was right. I was lonely for Bob and the things that we had shared. But it wasn't an existential kind of loneliness with the sense of being alone and incomplete. It was very specific, and nothing would change it. I didn't want anything to change it. Bob would be both happy and sad to know how much I missed him.

I cried one last time with this group that had watched me cry, as I had watched them, all year.

Finally, on this day, I planted a tree in Bob's memory. Sometimes Bob and I would drive through the countryside looking at houses or beaches or towns, and in a chorus we might say, "This is nice, but there are not enough trees." This one was for Bob. I stood at the nursery mulling over the choices. A pyracantha with red berries, like Bob's hair. A Japanese maple. A crabapple that would blossom in the spring. Bob would have liked them all. They were all half-price. I finally chose the crabapple. It would be easier to plant.

Trees. The symbol of life. On my college seal there is a tree, branches outstretched, filling the circle. Around the tree are the words, *That they may have life and have it abundantly.* Bob had life abundantly. So do I. Except for the bad times, it is okay.